DAVY CROCKETT

DAVY CROCKETT

★

by STEWART H. HOLBROOK

Illustrated by ERNEST RICHARDSON

RANDOM HOUSE · NEW YORK

For My Daughters

Sibyl Morningstar Holbrook

Bonnie Stewart Holbrook

CONTENTS

Foreword   ix

1. Hunting with a Flintlock   3
2. Davy, the Boy Drover   12
3. The Big Shooting Match   24
4. 105 Big Black Bears   35
5. Davy Crockett, Scout   48
6. The First Battle   60
7. The Fight at Talladega   73
8. Blood on the Tallapoosa   84
9. Life in The Shakes   97
10. Down the Big River   108
11. Friend of Indians   118
12. Colonel Crockett Goes West   132
13. The Lone Star Republic   143
14. A Hero of the Alamo   155

Memorials to Davy Crockett   169

Index   175

FOREWORD

The importance of Davy Crockett is less in what he did than in what he was. For more than two centuries after the founding of the first settlements in North America, the man who braved the frontier, who "opened up the country," was highly regarded. Toting a gun and an ax, he adventured into the wilderness to build a cabin, to hew out a clearing, and to plant a little corn. Then he moved on with the sun, always west.

No other time and place could have produced him. Europe was tamed and colonized by clans and tribes. America was tamed and settled by individuals. Men like Crockett moved alone, hunted alone, planted alone. Only in time of war did they join together. Then they went their several ways again.

These people did not like to have neighbors within sound of ax or gunshot. It made them feel crowded. So, Davy Crockett moved to make one clearing after another; he wanted his boys to grow up in an ever wilder country. Thousands more felt the same way. Among them all they turned savage lands into territories, then made the territories into states.

Crockett's intelligence, his wit, his all-around competence as a pioneer made him a perfect symbol of the restless people who were chasing the frontier from the Appalachians to the Pacific shore. He was kindly, big-hearted, poor in money and possessions, and wholly without fear—the perfect combination for a folk hero in the United States. That his death should have come as it did, his rifle blazing, defying an enemy that was trying to halt the advance of the American frontier, assured him the immortality which we Americans like to bestow upon our heroes.

Stewart Holbrook

DAVY CROCKETT

1

HUNTING WITH A FLINTLOCK

IT WAS GOING TO BE A DAY TO BE REMEMBERED IN
the young life of David Crockett. It was now
only a little past noon, and he could hardly
know that before dark he was going to take his
first shot at a bear. Davy was eight years and
two months old. For two months past he had
been allowed to take his father's gun and go

into the woods to hunt meat for the family table.

He had done pretty well at it, bringing home a big gray squirrel, or a possum, or perhaps a partridge. It was never more than one, for his father, John Crockett, had ruled that the lad should take with him only a single bullet and one charge of powder at a time. If he missed, as he sometimes did, and brought home no game at all, he had to go supperless to bed. This was the penalty for his poor marksmanship.

If it seems to us nowadays a cruel way to bring up a boy, we must remember that in Davy Crockett's time and place, there was nothing else so important to a man as knowing how to handle a rifle. If he also learned to read and write a bit, and perhaps how to cipher, as arithmetic was called, that was all right, too; but these things were not what gave a man something to eat, or protected his life in the backwoods of North America.

The Crockett rifle rested on wooden pegs in the wall above the fireplace. Standing on one of the stools that served as chairs, Davy took down the gun which was a good eighteen inches taller than his own four feet. It was of course a flintlock, and it worked in this way: When

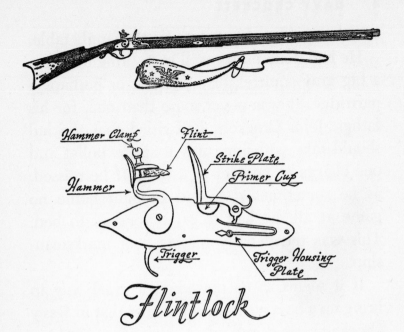

Flintlock

the trigger was pulled, a hammer holding a bit of hard stone called flint struck the steel powder pan; the resulting spark ignited a few specks of powder; the flash entered the gun through the touchhole, and the main charge of powder exploded and sent the bullet on its way.

Davy knew just how to load it. First he blew hard through the hole to make sure the barrel was clear. From the powder horn he poured a charge in at the muzzle, followed the powder with a small piece of rag, and with the iron ramrod pushed the whole charge down to the end of the barrel. Now he dropped a single lead ball and another rag into the barrel, and tamped them down firmly. Putting the long gun on the table, he filled the shallow firing pan with powder. He pushed a small feather through the touchhole to make sure it was clear. He tightened the screw that held the flint. He placed the hammer just right on the pan.

He was ready. He did not have far to go. The Crockett cabin stood in a small clearing in the middle of a wilderness which ran on and on for hundreds of miles.

With the long heavy rifle on one shoulder, and both hands holding the stock, the four-foot-tall hunter moved slowly and without noise into the twilight of the forest. He already knew these woods as today's boys and girls know the block in which they live. Today, Davy planned to follow a ridge where the beech trees stood big and tall. There was less brush here than on lower ground. It was easier to carry the gun. "I just might see me a bear," he thought, "though it ain't quite time for them to come and eat beechnuts." He noticed a few beech burs on the ground, but they were still green. No, it was too early.

The forest quiet was suddenly broken by a tremendous whir of wings. Davy was startled for a moment; then he relaxed, leaning on his rifle to watch one of the great sights of the southern woods. A hundred, maybe five hundred bright green birds rose from a big beech and flew around in circles. Chattering, screaming, and whistling, they made a noisy bedlam that included sounds much like human speech. Davy knew them to be Carolina parakeets, said to be the only species of the parrot family ever to invade the United States. He sat down to enjoy their gorgeous coloring, and tried to make out what they were saying.

"Maybe I can learn their language," Davy said aloud, the way people do who are much alone. The birds had now settled down in another tree and, still chattering, were eying the boy with interest. Davy let go a long low whistle. The chatter stopped instantly, then resumed, and a few of the birds came nearer. "They's too pretty to shoot," he thought, and he made a clucking noise. The parakeets loved it, and for perhaps an hour Davy forgot he was out to shoot for his supper. The birds remained near so long as he talked to them.

Rifle on shoulder, Davy moved on down the ridge, slowly, carefully. The sun was getting lower. The boy's eye ranged over the tall trees one after the other, seeking a squirrel. It would do, lacking bigger game like a possum, a raccoon, or—and it seemed too much to expect—a black bear. "When I've got me a bear," Davy told his rifle, "then I'll be a man. Nobody's a man who ain't shot a bear."

On went the boy hunter, working down a slope of the ridge toward the Limestone River. The brush grew thicker. When he came to a spot where he could see the sun, he noted it was later than he had thought. He'd spent too long watching and talking with those lovely green birds. Well, if he saw nothing to shoot at, he'd go home with a loaded rifle. He hated to return without a shot, but it was better that way than to shoot and miss—and get no supper.

The twilight of the woods was growing darker when Davy saw something moving in a clump of bushes. He stopped in his tracks. He took the rifle from his shoulder, cocked it, looked at the pan, and waited, his eye on the bushes. There—it moved again, whatever it was. And a moment later it stood up. Yes, stood up, for it was a bear, a black bear. The animal took one look at the boy, then it turned and started out of sight.

Davy's brief look at the animal told him this was not a grown bear. It was a cub, a big fat cub, but a cub. It was also the first time Davy had ever seen a bear when he had a gun in his hands. He raised the rifle, took quick aim, and fired.

Through the billowing blue smoke Davy saw a huge black form seem to rise up straight out of the ground and charge toward him. It was a she-bear, a big one, and she was as angry as any animal can get. She was coming fast, too, for once she saw the boy she dropped to her four feet and started for him almost as fast as a deer could run.

The young hunter stood frozen, motionless. What to do? He could not have loaded again even if he had powder. Should he stand and fight with his gun for a club? Or what?

In the split second while these thoughts raced through the boy's mind, the cub gave a long whine, almost like a baby's. The mother bear paused in her charge, to see what was the matter with her child. It was only a pause, but it was long enough for Davy. Still clinging fast to the long rifle, he took off as fast as he could run. As luck had it, the ground was downhill.

The she-bear paused as the cub gave a long whine.

A man can beat a bear running downhill, and Davy Crockett ran away from the angered she-bear.

Arriving home out of breath and excited, the lad was also filled with shame. He should have known better than to shoot at a cub.

His father had no pity. "Did you kill the cub?" he asked.

"No," said Davy, "I missed him." He knew it was no use to ask his father if he was to have supper that night.

Without another word Davy cleaned the rifle, put it back on the pegs over the fireplace, then crawled silently up the ladder to his bed of boughs under the eaves. He was hungry, and it would be a long time until breakfast. But he knew he deserved the punishment for two reasons: (1) He had been so foolish as to shoot at a cub; (2) he had brought home nothing to eat.

Such were the early experiences of the boy who was to become the most celebrated frontier character in the United States.

2

DAVY, THE BOY DROVER

PERHAPS GOING TO BED WITHOUT SUPPER HELPS TO make a dead shot and a good all-around woodsman. But there is more to it than that. This boy, who with a long heavy rifle was hunting alone at the age of eight, was born of two generations who had spent their lives in the wilderness.

Grandfather David Crockett emigrated from Ireland to America before the Revolution. He settled in the forested back country of Carolina where he raised a large family. Both he and his son John fought with Americans during the Revolutionary War, and at war's end both families moved over the mountains into what was then called the State of Franklin. (In 1796 it was admitted into the Union as the State of Tennessee.)

The end of the war did not bring peace to the State of Franklin. This was the frontier. Violence followed the frontier as it moved toward the sun. Without warning, one day in 1786, a band of roving Indians swept into the clearing made by David Crockett in the Nolachucky Valley, set the cabin afire, and massacred almost the entire family.

Why the Indians did not attack the home of John Crockett, only a few miles from his father's place, was never explained. It was here on August 17th, only a short time after the massacre at the elder Crockett's, that a ninth child was born to John and Rebecca Crockett. He was named David for his grandfather. This child was to become the famous Davy Crockett. Like his grandfather, he too was to die of violence, but not before he had lived for fifty years a life of adventure such as comes to few men.

Davy Crockett's training for life in frontier America started, as already related, at a tender age. His was a hard boyhood even in that rough-and-tumble time. His father was a shiftless man who always owed somebody money. The little gristmill he built was a failure, and when high water washed it down the river, he simply moved a few miles farther on where a trail forded the Holston River.

There John Crockett built a large cabin, nailed up a few extra bunks, and called the place a tavern. He had hay and corn to feed a traveler's horse, pork and potatoes to feed the traveler himself, and a variety of game. The nine children must have provided all the help he needed, but even so, John Crockett was always in need of a few more dollars than he had.

In that day it was a custom in many large families to "bind out" a son or daughter to work at a trade or on a farm. That was what happened to young Davy Crockett. The year he was twelve—by then he had killed an even dozen bears, none of them cubs—his father bound him out to work for a German farmer named Jacob Siler who happened to stop overnight at the Crockett tavern.

Because the farmer had come to Tennessee to buy and drive cattle back over the mountains to his farm in Virginia's Shenandoah Valley, Davy started work as a drover. His pay for the trip was to be six dollars. For almost 400 miles he and the German drove a sizable herd of cattle over muddy trails, across rivers, and through swamps, often sleeping by the wayside, and finally came to the fine country of the Shenandoah.

The German paid Davy the six dollars agreed upon, but told the lad he should continue to work for him on the farm.

Davy stayed and worked. He didn't like cattle, or hay, or anything about farming. He stayed only because he didn't know any better, and because he was afraid the German would have him arrested if he didn't stay. But meanwhile he was planning how best to get away. Luck was with him. He got to talking with a band of wagoners, whose wagons were loaded with flour and molasses and who were heading west over the mountains for Tennessee. There they would sell their cargoes, load up with corn, and return.

One of the wagon drivers looked familiar to Davy. Like most of his kind he was a rough and jolly fellow, given to jokes and much loud talk, proud of his job, proud of the whip he carried and of his knowledge of the country beyond the mountains.

Davy stepped boldly up to the wagoner. "Did you," he asked, "ever stop at John Crockett's place?"

"You mean John Crockett who runs the tavern on the Holston?" said the wagoner.

"Yes. He's my father."

"Sure, I remember. You're the young feller that shot us a fine mess of partridge last time I was there."

Davy was delighted. "I want to go home," he said. Then he explained how he had been bound out to the German farmer. "I stayed my time," said Davy, "but he won't let me go. I'm going to leave him."

The other drivers gathered around. They agreed it would be a fine idea for Davy to go home. "We'll get you there," one of the men said, "or pretty near there, anyway. We'll hit the Holston a few miles above your place. You can get the rest of the way easy." He told Davy the wagoners were to make camp that night at a spot about seven miles beyond the German's farm. "You get there by daybreak," he told Davy. "We'll have something for you to eat, then we'll all go over the mountains together."

Over the mountains! That's where he wanted to go. Over to the other side of the mountains. The boy honestly believed that he wanted to go home, but it is more likely he simply wanted to go somewhere else from where he was. It was in his blood. To go over to the other side of the mountains—that was music, it was poetry, it was life.

Luck was still with young Davy. That evening Mr. Siler and his family drove off to stay overnight with friends, leaving Davy alone on the farm. Well, this was his chance!

Young Crockett never closed an eye that night. It could have been a little after midnight when he got up. He already had put his few extra clothes and what little money he had in a bundle under the bed. It was cold in the house, and dark. The fireplace glowed from a few embers which he stirred before warming a slab of cornbread on the small ash-shovel.

It wasn't much of a breakfast for a healthy boy, but he thought it would do until he got to the teamsters' camp.

He looked out the small window. Everything was white. It must have been snowing since early evening. But, snow or not, he must be on his way. Seven miles was quite a piece.

He put a short stick through the knot of his bundle, opened the door, and stepped out into eight inches of new snow. More was still falling. If the wind had been blowing, he thought, he would call it a blizzard. But this was fine and dandy. The blanket of soft white made him think that snow somehow changed things and made a new world out of an old one. From far off came the muffled call of an owl.

By the time he had got to what was called the Big Road, the one used by wagoners, Davy found himself in a real blizzard. The snow was deeper, too. He plowed ahead steadily, but more slowly now. Every little while he bumped into an old stump; that meant he had got off the road. He wasn't discouraged, for it made him glad to think that his tracks would be covered as fast as he made them. "Old Siler won't be able to follow me," he thought.

After what seemed an age, Davy saw a light

not far ahead. It was the wagoners' campfire. Daylight was more than an hour away but the men were stirring. They gave Davy a thumping big breakfast, and then the wagon train got going, heading for the mountains and Tennessee.

The snow grew deeper, yet the wheels kept turning. Many days later the wagons went up steeper grades and over the mountains. The going was better. Davy stayed with the party until they were within some fifteen miles of John Crockett's tavern. Then he bade his jolly friends the wagoners good-by, and struck out on foot. He was soon home, but apparently there was no rejoicing. "My father," Davy said, "greeted me without surprise."

For a week or so Davy attended the new school near by. He soon got into a scrape of some sort with the schoolmaster, who threatened to report the youth to John Crockett. Davy did not go home that day. He walked down the river a mile or so to a place where a drover, taking cattle east to Virginia, had camped for the night.

Davy bound himself to the drover, and next day was on his way back to Virginia again, driving cattle over the Blue Ridge Mountains and on to Front Royal, away up in northern Virginia. After he had got his pay, Davy took another job. This time he drove a wagon in a train going to a city he had heard of, Baltimore, in Maryland.

Baltimore was then one of the biggest cities in the United States. Young Crockett was bugeyed at the tall buildings, as many as four stories high, and the crowds of people on the streets. A score of ships at the docks caught his eye, and for a time he thought he'd like to go to sea. Nothing came of the idea. He left Baltimore with another wagon train and, when that trip was done, took a job working for a hatter. A few weeks later the hatter skipped the country, owing everybody including Davy, who lost out on the wages due him.

Penniless, and in a strange country, Davy again took work that he hated, which was farming. This time he got his wages, and at once struck forth again. He would return to Tennessee for good.

But his trip over the Blue Ridge brought Davy more hardship than he had ever experienced before. Having found a canoe on the bank of a river, he got in and cast off, only to discover that this body of water was wilder than any he had seen on the Holston. In no time at all the craft was half filled with water. She was hard to manage, and by the time Davy got her to shore, he was not only wet through but his clothes had frozen so stiff he could hardly move.

Luckily, he landed not far from a cabin. The people living in it made him welcome, fed him, and let him thaw out by the fire. He set out again next day in the foothills of the Blue Ridge. It was, he remembered, as lonely a trail as he ever walked. There was not a cabin anywhere, and the few wagons he met were all going east. He spent his last few cents to buy some bread from a wagoner, and when that was gone he had nothing to eat.

It came to Davy's mind that he must be getting soft. Buying bread when the woods were alive with game on every side! Spotting some wild grapes near the trail, he made a neat snare from a length of the tough grapevine, and set it across a well-worn runway. He'd have a rabbit in the morning, he was certain. And he did. He skinned it deftly, then built a fire with the flint and steel he carried, and cooked and ate the animal.

This was the way for a man to live! Let the

forest feed him. City people might buy bread. Not woodsmen!

Now that he was back in his own country, Davy felt better. He had no gun, but for the rest of the way home he lived well on rabbits he snared, and on trout he caught with his hands. He had changed, however, in the two years he had been roaming. The family did not recognize him when he walked into the tavern. When they did, his father John had an idea. It had to do, naturally, with his need for money. He told Davy he must work six months for a neighbor, Abraham Wilson, to pay off a debt of thirty-six dollars the elder Crockett owed him. If he would do this, his father promised, the boy could go on his own hook. In other words, he would then be free to do as he pleased.

It was farm work, but Davy stuck it out and thus paid his father's debt. Then came a disagreeable surprise. His father owed another debt, this one to a Quaker, John Kennedy, who had a farm in the neighborhood. Would he please go work for the Quaker? It wasn't fair, but Davy, who liked the Quaker, agreed and went to work. The Quaker liked Davy, too. He supplied the youth with the only good suit of clothes he had ever had. He also sent him to school for several months. Davy didn't know it then, in fact he was anything but happy in school, yet those few weeks of reading, writing and figuring were to be of the greatest importance to him later on.

3

THE BIG SHOOTING MATCH

DAVY FOUND QUAKER KENNEDY VERY DIFFERENT from any other employer he had known. This kindly man took a real interest in the youth, helping him with his school work when need be, never demanding more labor than he had a right to expect. When he had worked out his father's debt, Davy was glad to stay on working and living with the Quaker.

Six months of school gave the boy a new interest. He read a number of books that belonged to his employer. He discovered that he had a really excellent memory; he could reel off whole pages, word for word, and within a little while he was delivering orations as he milked the cows. His writing, too, came more easily now.

Though the Quaker gave Davy every encouragement, he also objected mildly to what he thought were Davy's bad habits. Like every other young person in the neighborhood, Davy enjoyed dances and all kinds of frolics. Working-bees were a common frontier custom. The backwoods people traded work. Neighbors would gather to help with the harvest at one farm, then at another. Putting up a new barn at a "raising" was almost a holiday, what with the womenfolk preparing huge quantities of food that was served on a long timber for a table, and the meal made jolly by fiddling, solo songs, and chorus singing.

Davy never missed a barn raising, nor a cornhusking, nor a logrolling. He was present at every flax-pulling and at every dance. Dances seldom broke up until dawn. "I fear," the old Quaker told him sadly, "I fear thee is bound to be a rolling stone." Davy didn't deny it. He enjoyed being a rolling stone. Had he not already rolled across the mountains and even seen the big city of Baltimore? He'd choose, if he had his way, to roll some more.

The lad had grown into a young man now. Tall and dark, with fine eyes and always a ready laugh, he was as slim and graceful as a sapling. All the boys liked him. So did all the girls, one of whom, a plump blonde maid, he had come to like best to dance with. He had even mentioned marriage. She said she was willing. So, one fine Sunday, he dressed in his best and only suit of clothes and walked ten miles to the cabin where she lived, with the idea of asking her to name the day. Here he got the shock of his young life. The fickle young woman was planning to be married next day to another man.

Stories have made out that Davy was terribly hurt. Maybe he was. If so, he recovered quickly and was soon keeping company with Polly Finlay, a neighbor's daughter. She too was fair-haired, and her eyes were as blue as cornflowers.

Now Davy began to think seriously of marriage. But he had no money. To get married, a man ought to have a little, or so he had been told. Davy had won many small prizes at shooting matches. Notice of by far the biggest match the neighborhood had ever known had just been posted in John Crockett's tavern. It was to be open to all comers. The first prize was a prime beef critter. That was something —a whole live steer. You could sell a steer. Davy had his name added to the list of men who were to take part.

The big event brought men carrying rifles from all over the neighborhood and from points twenty-five miles away. They numbered more than eighty, and in age from eighteen to seventy years. This was shooting country. Whoever won this match was certain to be a dead shot.

The shooting was done at homemade targets each with three circles and a bull's-eye in the center. The distance started at fifty yards. Each man was allowed only one shot. The three top marksmen—or more, if some were tied—then shot at seventy-five yards; and again, in the finals, at one hundred yards. Davy was to use John Crockett's rifle, the same he had carried when he shot game at the age of eight. He knew the gun well. He called her Old Betsy.

The day was cloudy, and without wind—perfect weather for match shooting. Off in a small field near the rifle range stood the first prize, a big, red Durham steer, eating grass, paying no heed to the men who had come to contend for the honor of leading him home. The three judges, or umpires, all wearing tall beaver hats with dignity, attempted to quiet the children, mostly boys, who were running and yelling, playing games, and probably fraying the nerves of the marksmen.

Shooting began. Davy was not surprised to hear the head judge announce that no less than forty-odd marksmen were tied for the top three places at fifty yards, among them Davy himself. But seventy-five yards finished off all but three. The marks of Davy, of an old backwoodsman named Clark, and a professional hunter, Milo Johnson, all were clustered within the black bull's-eye.

"The gentlemen will now shoot it out at one hundred yards," cried the chief judge. "In a minute, Crockett, Clark and Johnson will draw straws. Long straw gets first crack. Shortest straw gets last chance."

Davy was cleaning his barrel, measuring

powder, inspecting the lead bullet. "I have got to win this time," he was telling himself. "I've just got to win."

The judges stepped off what they said was one hundred yards, and a fresh target was set up. The circles and the bull's-eyes looked much smaller at the new distance.

"Gentlemen, will you now draw for your place?"

The three men stepped up. Clark got the longest straw, Davy the shortest.

"Mr. Clark, get ready."

The lean, grizzled old man looked to be seventy years of age. He might have been seventy-five. But he stepped quickly up to the little stake driven in the ground, raised his eyes to the target, raised his rifle with a slow, easy sweep, and took aim. The sharp crack was still echoing around the hills when the judges called the hit. "Bull's-eye!" The crowd yelled and someone cried: "Old Clark, he's from old Kaintuck and they don't shoot no better than him!"

"Are you ready, Mr. Johnson?"

Johnson was ready. But although he was younger than Clark, he moved more slowly. Davy thought the man took a mighty long time to get his sights on the mark. Then he fired.

"Bull's-eye!" the judges shouted. The crowd made more noise.

"Davy Crockett, ready." The judges thought Davy too young to be called "mister."

Slim, tall Davy took his place. In one graceful quick motion he brought Old Betsy to his shoulder, sighted for the fraction of a second, and fired.

It was another bull's-eye! The crowd went wild. Yes, sir, this was shooting country.

The judge at last made himself heard above the din. "The three Nimrods will shoot again at a new target, same distance," he said.

This time something must have happened to the old backwoodsman's eye or nerves. His bullet hit within the smallest circle but missed the bull's-eye. It was now a match between Johnson and Davy.

Again the deliberate hunter stepped to the mark. Ever so slowly he raised his gun. Then he sighted—and sighted some more while a tense silence fell over the watchers. Then, just before he pulled the trigger, the quiet was broken by a startling bellow. The first prize was thirsty. He wanted water. And, in the manner of beef critters, he called for water in the only way he knew. He bellowed.

The crowd, so tense a moment before, broke into laughter. Either the bellow or the laughter was too much for marksman Johnson. His arm must have faltered just a little, for his bullet merely nicked the edge of the black spot that was the bull's-eye.

Still, considering the distance and the size of the target, Johnson's shot was better than good. After all, old Clark, whose nerves were like steel, had wholly missed the bull's-eye. Marksman Davy Crockett would have to be better than good to beat Johnson's shot. He knew it, too, but he didn't admit as much to himself. What he did was to brag to himself. As he carefully poured a few grains of powder into Old Betsy's powder pan, he muttered: "I can hit that bull's-eye while laying on my back, or hanging by my heels from a hickory limb. I can hit that mark with one eye shut and a bug in my other eye. I can . . ."

"Davy Crockett, ready."

A quick stride and he was at the mark. He raised the rifle with the same sweeping movement as before. He squinted along the barrel

—hoping the prize steer would remain quiet
—and pulled the stock snug against his shoulder. His right eye saw the little bead on the
end of the gun swing slowly. His finger tightened on the trigger. When the bead swung
fair against the back of the target, Davy pulled.
The smoke was still hanging in the still air
when the judge shouted, "Bull's-eye!"

Men and boys crowded around to shake
Davy's hand, to slap his back, and to tell one
another that Tennessee was shooting country
and Davy Crockett was the shootingest man in
Tennessee.

Now that it was over, the young marksman's hands were shaking just a little. But he
was wildly happy. He had showed himself to
be the best shot along the Holston River and
for twenty miles back on each bank. Even
better, he was offered five gold dollars for his
prize steer. Davy took the money so fast it was
hot, he said, when he put it in his pocket.

The shooting match was on a Saturday. On
Sunday Davy again put on his one good suit
of clothes, a new coonskin cap with tail hanging down, and walked to the Finlay place. Polly
knew he would come. With blue cornflowers
in her fair hair she was sitting in the swing

"Bull's-eye!" called the judges as the crowd roared.

under the big gum tree. Davy lost no time. Within five minutes Polly had said yes, she would like to be Mrs. Davy Crockett.

Yet the matter was not finished. When they went hand in hand into the house, and told Polly's mother the news, she stood up tall and grim, and her mouth closed on every word like a steel trap. "No," said Mrs. Finlay, "you will not marry my daughter."

"But why not?" pleaded Davy.

The woman would give no reason. She sent Polly to her bedroom, then told Davy she would excuse him if he went back home, where he belonged.

The champion marksman, a five-dollar gold piece still in his pocket, returned to the Quaker's place and went to bed without a word. The world was, after all, a pretty terrible place.

4

105 BIG BLACK BEARS

YET THINGS WERE NOT NEARLY SO TERRIBLE AS they seemed to Davy, who was trying to forget Mrs. Finlay's strong hint that he had better not see Polly any more.

Even while he tossed on his bed, Polly and her father were working hard on Mrs. Finlay, whose eyes were wet with tears.

"But Polly is only seventeen," she protested.

Mr. Finlay laughed. "And," he asked, "how old were *you* when you married me?"

Mrs. Finlay didn't answer. She only cried some more.

Polly spoke up. "How old *was* she, Pa?"

"She lacked five months of being seventeen."

"What?" cried Polly. "Mother was only *six*teen?" She said "six" as loud as she could.

"That's a fact, my girl. Your mother was only seven months more than *six*teen years old."

"But, but, but . . ." Mrs. Finlay was trying to think of something to say.

"Davy Crockett is a good boy," Mr. Finlay said.

"Yes, I know that." She was weakening now. "I'd rather our Polly married him than any other boy in the whole country."

It was nearly over now. Mr. Finlay winked at Polly. Polly smiled. They let Mrs. Finlay talk. She was feeling much better. Yes, Davy Crockett was a nice boy—and so on and so on. Father and daughter did not try to hurry her. They knew the signs. Let her sleep on it. Morning would find everything as right as could be.

Two weeks later, Davy and Polly were married in the Finlay cabin. Then the wedding party, which meant almost everybody in the neighborhood, hastened to John Crockett's tavern for the dance that lasted until roosters were crowing.

Quaker Kennedy gave the couple a credit order on the crossroads store for fifteen dollars. In those days, fifteen dollars would buy a lot. Davy still had the five-dollar gold piece he had won with Old Betsy. And Mrs. Finlay gave the couple two fine cows and their new calves, as well as Polly's spinning wheel and loom. These the bride took with her to the cabin with a garden in a small clearing Davy had rented for one year for twenty-five cents a month.

A year or so was long enough. The old Quaker had been right. Davy Crockett was a rolling stone. The love of far places was in his blood. Only he never put it that way. "I want my children to grow up in new country," he said. He and Polly already had a baby boy.

Day by day the urge grew stronger. "I hear there's some fine wild land down in South Tennessee," he told Polly again and again. "We can have it for the taking." And he talked and talked, breaking down the fear Polly had of travel. After all, she had never been more than ten miles from where she was born. Davy, of course, was a much traveled man. He continued to tell Polly about the wonderful country of southern Tennessee. He had never been there, but he already talked as if he owned it.

"There's the best hunting in the world down there," he told his wife.

"How far is it from here?"

"Oh, not very far. A week or so of good smart travel ought to get us there."

"How do we get there—by walkin'?"

"No, sir. We'll take one of the boats on the river. When there's a stream, that's the best way."

"Might get drownded."

"Polly, I can swim like the best alligator you've ever seen. I'll put you and the baby on my back. Pile on the wheel and the loom. Pack on a hundred pounds of vittles. And the dogs will swim right alongside me. No danger at all, Polly."

"Aren't we goin' to take the hosses?"

"Oh, sure. I forgot about the hosses. They probably can swim almost as good as me."

Spring, when the water was high, was the best time, and when it came around the next

year, Davy and Polly packed their household
gear on two colts. By this time a second baby
boy had been born in the Crockett household.
On the trip Polly carried the children and rode
the old horse. Davy carried his gun. At his heels
went his hunting dogs. They went to the nearest boat station on the Holston, getting there
just in time to see a big boat tying up at the
landing.

"My!" cried wide-eyed Polly. "It must be as
big as the Ark in the Bible."

"An ark, that's what they call it," said Davy.
"It's just a big flatboat. Not much like the ships
I saw in Baltimore, but I reckon it'll get us
there."

"Hey Captain," Davy called to one of the
crew who looked like the boss. "You got room
for us?"

"Sure have. Take the whole pack and passel
of you. Best boat on the river, too."

The ark was a good sixty feet long, square
nosed, built of thick planks. A little back from
her middle was a small house, on the roof of
which stood the pilot who steered her with a
long single oar called a sweep. She carried a
small sail to help when she came upriver—an

"You got room for us?" Davy shouted to the captain.

aid to the crew who plied her with oars and pikepoles against the current. Going downriver all she needed was the current.

In the cabin were bunks. Davy led the three horses to the deck behind the cabin and tethered them. The household gear was stowed on the forward deck. The Crocketts were the first to get aboard. But they were not to be the only passengers. Within a few minutes a family consisting of father, mother, and six children, together with their horses, a cow, and a crate of chickens, were taken on. A little later two men in buckskin shirts, carrying rifles and bundles of coonskins and other furs, got on. Then five men began loading hardwood staves—hundreds and hundreds of them—until the foredeck rose higher as the ark sank deeper in the water.

Away they went down the winding Holston River. The current was swift, the water was high, and everything went famously. Polly and Davy, with the babies in Polly's arms, sat on the roof of the cabin, their legs dangling, watching with fascination the scenes that changed so rapidly. The red maples were in full bud. The tall hemlocks and pines dipped and waved as if in salute to the travelers. Grassy valleys came into view. Foaming creeks rushed to join the river. Here and there stood a deer to peer wonderingly at the boat; flocks of startled ducks rose from the stream.

On went the river, and on went the boat, day and night, stopping only at a few settlements where perhaps half a dozen passengers were added to the company. The captain told them the cabin was full, and they would have to sleep on deck.

Then they came to the great, broad silvery Tennessee River, beside which the Holston seemed only a brook. Even Davy admitted that here was a queen among rivers. But they were now near the end of their journey. At a place where only a long rambling cabin stood by the river bank, the ark swung in and the Crocketts went ashore. From here a rough trail led over the mountains and down into the Elk River country which is now Lincoln County, Tennessee.

With Davy walking ahead, Polly and the babies on the old horse, and the two colts and their loads bringing up the rear, the Crockett caravan started west up the trail. The dogs were crazy with excitement, after their long confinement on the ark. They ran barking ahead, then back, chasing birds, inspecting everything.

The hounds were no happier than their master. "I'm a rolling stone," Davy sang as he moved along with long strides, "I'm a rolling stone, I'm rolling home." New country. More bears. More bees. More timber. More cougars. Sweet grass in the clearings.

The weather was fine. They camped nights beside the trail, cooking racoons and squirrels Davy shot along the way. Three days brought them to the head of Mulberry Fork of Elk River. This was the place; and in a grassy clearing surrounded by gums and beeches and maples and pines Davy built a small cabin. It didn't have windows. Its floor was the ground. "But we'll have some bearskin rugs soon enough," Davy told Polly. "Plenty of bear sign in this country."

The Crocketts were in time for planting. They'd have potatoes and green stuff and corn and gourds by late summer. Meanwhile they would get their fill of bear meat and venison and possum and coon. Yes, and wild honey. Within the first week Davy made a fire at the foot of a broken old tree, and covered the fire with green grass until smoke billowed everywhere. Then he chopped down the tree, and while hundreds of bees buzzed with fury, only to fly away or to die in the thick smoke, Davy gathered almost one hundred pounds of honey. "Nary a sting," he told Polly. "Some tried to, but they gave it up when they found how tough I was."

The bears were as thick as Davy hoped. The woods were alive with big wild turkeys, birds that weighed up to thirty pounds. There were plenty of racoons; also the racoons' enemy, the oppossum. Davy Crockett did as little farming as possible. He didn't have time. In twelve months he killed 105 black bears. He never counted the coons, possums, turkeys and deer that fell to his gun.

Davy's kill of bears was a record for Tennessee. News of it spread out over the trails and streams. Word got around that there was a young woodsman on Mulberry Fork who shot enough bear meat to feed every soul in Lincoln County, and enough coons to make caps for every man, boy and child above five years of age in the state.

The stories about Davy Crockett started big and grew bigger. Half the time, it was told, he didn't trouble to shoot a treed coon down; he *grinned* him down. He simply twisted his face and mouth to look like the coons' hated enemy, the possum. Then he grinned and grinned and grinned. The coon got so mad he came bounding down out of the tree—and Davy grabbed him.

This Davy Crockett—so the stories had it— never had a canoe. When he wanted to get across the Mulberry, or to get downriver a piece, or upriver a piece, he simply "grinned" an alligator. "I like to have a fine big 'gator sunning himself on a log," one of the stories quoted Davy. "I reach out with my rifle and just tap his snout a bit—wake him up. He opens

"I jumps on his back a-straddle and away we go!"

one eye, cocks it at me, then I begin to grin
him. I grin him till he flops into the water and
comes over. 'Mister,' I tell him, 'I want to get
down to the Forks quick. Give me a ride.' I
jumps on his back a-straddle, and away we go
skimming downriver thirty mile an hour. It's a
right good way to travel, too."

It was just as well that Davy Crockett got
his fun now, for his country was going to need
men like Davy, and need them badly. Word
about this need was coming over the mountains, following the rivers, moving up the creeks,
finally getting to the last cabin in the remotest
mountain valley. It was the year 1812, and the
United States and Great Britain were at war
again.

That was bad enough. What made matters worse, so far as the South was concerned, was that the British were stirring up the Indians to attack American settlements. A Shawnee leader named Tecumseh was moving into Tennessee, into Mississippi Territory, arousing the Creeks, telling them to kill or drive out the white people. If they didn't do so now, he told them, they would never have another chance.

Tecumseh himself was killed in the northern fighting, but one of his lieutenants led the Creeks in an attack on Fort Mims, in what is now Alabama. A whole settlement of white men and women, together with their children, was massacred.

News of the tragedy traveled swiftly throughout the country. It reached the Crockett home early one evening by way of a trapper who had got it from a storekeeper at Winchester, the trading center. It gave Davy something to think about besides hunting.

Next morning at breakfast, Polly and the boys wondered what was the matter. Davy was sober and serious, in contrast to his usual fun-loving self. Polly guessed what was troubling him, and soon enough she knew for sure.

"Polly," he said, "I've often heard people tell

about war. I've never seen any war. I never thought I could fight that way. But you know what happened at the fort. It was wicked. I must go."

Polly cried a little. Then the boys cried. Davy comforted the children. "It will only be a little while," he told them. "Polly, my Grandpa Crockett fought the redcoats at King's Mountain long afore I was born. So did my father. They were both good shots. I've got a better gun than they had, and I'm a better shot, too. I'm going downriver and see if our country can use another sharpshooter."

When the hounds saw Davy come outside, long rifle over his shoulder, they began to leap and howl and laugh and bark. This time, however, they could not go. One after the other, Davy called to them. He called them by name, names that were to become famous all over the United States. "Here Whirlwind, here Soundwell and Growler. Come Holdfast, come Deathmaul, come Grim . . ." Giving each a pat, he ordered them into the house. Then he kissed Polly and the boys, and started down the winding trail toward Winchester. Davy Crockett was off to war.

5

DAVY CROCKETT, SCOUT

DAVY CROCKETT—HERE HE WAS ALREADY IN enemy country, scouting ahead of a little band of volunteers in command of Major William Russell. Less than a week before, Davy had left Polly and the children and the woods that he knew so well.

Now he moved ahead with caution. This

Mississippi Territory, a part of which was to become the state of Alabama, was all new to him, as it was to the others; and the safety of the thirty-five volunteers depended a great deal on Scout Crockett.

They were heading for the camp where General Andrew Jackson was collecting an army to subdue the rampaging Creeks who had massacred the white people at Fort Mims.

Late in the first afternoon of the march, Davy was passing along the edge of an opening in thick timber. The woods had been unusually quiet for a mile or two. He hadn't heard any birds. Well, maybe down here in the Territory the birds were different. Perhaps they didn't chipper and call late in the day.

Davy moved ahead, his moccasined feet as quiet as the pads of a cougar. He kept carefully out of the opening. He had almost got around it when the hush was suddenly broken by the quick clatter of a squirrel's call. Davy stopped short. He peered across the opening from where the noise came.

"That doesn't sound just right," he told himself. "It's not the kind of squirrel I know, anyway." But if it were an animal, he wanted to see it. He stepped nearer the opening.

As Davy stood looking into the clearing he could see no sign of beast or man. "Queer," he thought. Then, as quick as lightning, he fell to one knee, just as a low whistling cut the silence. From behind him came a thud. He glanced up and back. There, in the trunk of a big pine four feet away, was an arrow, its feathered shaft quivering.

At the same instant, quick-thinking Davy Crockett let go a long cry that ended in deep moaning. Still on one knee, he cocked Old Betsy—and waited. Nothing happened. He groaned again, this time not so loud as before, and let the sound die in a gasp. With one eye peering through bushes toward the far side of the opening, Davy waited—and waited. All was complete silence.

Then, from around one side of a large rock on the far side of the opening, came a face the color of copper. Davy Crockett's right forefinger went tight. Betsy roared. The copper face disappeared. A cloud of smoke rolled out from Davy's bush to hang over the clearing.

"I sure got him," Davy thought. "But there are more of 'em around here." Yet the hush was so intense Davy could feel it. The little noise he made reloading could not have been heard two feet distant. "But the boys must have heard me shoot. It'll give 'em warning."

It did, too. A couple of hundred yards back, Major Russell and thirty-three volunteers stopped the moment Crockett fired. "Boys," said the Major, "Davy's run into something. Maybe it's meat for supper. But it could be something else. Keep your guns ready. Follow me." The band strung out in single file, the men walking twenty feet apart. They moved ahead in the direction where Davy still crouched in the bushes, waiting, watching.

Slowly, silently, Davy backed away from the clearing, then started to circle around it. On the far side, near the big rock, he stopped. Lying flat on his stomach, bow still in one hand, was a half-naked Indian. Davy noted the charm ornaments around the neck and arms of the dead man. "Creek," he thought. Then Davy turned and walked briskly back to meet Major Russell.

"What happened?" asked the Major.

Davy told him. "What I'm scared of, Major," he said, "is that this varmint is only one of a whole band of 'em. This is hot war country we're in."

"Let's see the one you got."

"I think he's a Creek," Davy said, leading his companions to the big boulder.

Major Russell bent to look closely. "Yes, he's a Creek, and that paint on his face and body means he was out for blood."

"I reckon his friends took off when they saw what happened to him," said Davy. "But we better be careful."

Taking counsel, Major Russell and his men decided to move on to the nearest spring and camp without fires for the night. After a meal of jerked meat, four guards were posted and the other men lay down to sleep. The night passed without event. So did the day. With Davy still scouting in advance, Major Russell and his party arrived in less than twenty hours more at the spot on a high bluff overlooking the Tennessee River where all volunteers were to meet.

It looked to Davy like a good place for a soldiers' camp. No enemy could attack it without being seen first. "But where's all the army?" Davy asked of Colonel John Coffee, camp commander. Davy could see less than a hundred men besides his own and Major Russell's party.

"They are coming, never fear," Colonel Coffee said. "And General Andrew Jackson is bringing them. A scout came this morning with word the General had been delayed."

Both Davy and Major Russell liked the look of Colonel Coffee. "He's got a real fighting face," Crockett said. He and Russell watched while the white-haired officer directed volunteers in digging latrines, cutting and piling fuel to be ready for the main army, and pitching the few tents available. Crockett wasn't mistaken about Coffee. The old Colonel had fought both British and Mohawks during the Revolution.

Later in the day, Coffee came to talk with Russell and Scout Crockett. "We got another message from the General," he told them. "Troops are coming both by the river and overland. They'll begin to arrive tomorrow. What the General doesn't know is that no provisions have arrived."

"Nothing to eat here?"

"Only a few barrels of flour, a bushel of salt, and a hogshead of molasses."

"No meat?" Crockett asked.

"Nary a bit. A drove of cattle is on the way —somewhere."

"A man can't fight without a little meat," said Crockett. "I can get some."

"Meat? What? Where?"

"I saw signs of bear not far from here."

"Bear would be better than nothing."

"Better than nothing?" repeated Davy. "There *isn't* any better meat if you cook it right."

"The men are going to be pretty hostile if we have no meat here."

"Say the word, Colonel, and I'll get you some meat."

"Davy Crockett, I've heard you were the greatest bear hunter in Tennessee, and . . ."

"Colonel," Davy broke in, "that's a lie. I'm the greatest bear hunter on earth."

"Prove it, then. Go get us a couple of big ones."

"Come on, Major. Let's take three or four of our boys to help with the lugging."

Crockett, Russell, and four of their scouts left camp and disappeared in the woods east of the river. They were still somewhere in the woods a day later when the first companies of militia arrived overland a little after daylight. They were still in the woods at noon when another 500 men, mixed militia and volunteers, hove in on flat boats and scows. They were absent around four o'clock when General Jackson, Old Hickory himself, came down the river in a big long ark, its decks covered with horses.

Colonel Coffee and other officers were there to greet the tall, sandy-haired and tough-looking commander of this army of Tennesseeans who were gathering to punish the Indians for the massacre at Fort Mims. General Jackson was not well. He was also suffering from a wound, not from an Indian but from a duel with a political enemy. One arm was in a sling.

"I'm late, Colonel," said Jackson. "And I apologize. It took a sore lot longer than need be to collect enough guns and powder to start this expedition."

Men were moving in long lines from the boats up to the camp site on top of the bluff. Each man had a small keg of powder on his shoulder. Other men were struggling with boxes of heavy flints.

"We've got plenty of shooting material," General Jackson went on, "but we look to be starvation poor for eating."

Colonel Coffee knew he might as well tell the General the bad news now. "General Jackson, the provisions haven't come. Nor word of them, either."

The weather-beaten face of Old Hickory

turned savage. He roared in his anger. Then he calmed down. "All right, Colonel, we'll eat molasses and salt."

The General and his officers went up the hill to camp and to the tent that had been prepared for headquarters. Jackson hurriedly wrote an order demanding to know what had happened to the supplies of food. "Take this to Lieutenant Stevens," he told his aide. "Tell him to give it to the two best canoe men he has. Let them paddle like the very devil upriver till they meet a long scow with the American flag on it. That's our provision boat. Give this message to the captain of the scow."

The sun was sinking as General Jackson and his officers completed their tour of the camp and walked back toward the headquarters tent. Just then a hullabaloo broke out at the north end of camp. There were shouts and yells as if Indians were attacking. Then came the thudding of drums, and high above them the shrill music of fifes.

"What's this all about?" Jackson scowled.

Colonel Coffee dared to guess, but not aloud. "I haven't the least idea, sir."

The drumming came nearer. The fifes broke

Hanging head down from each pole was a black bear.

into a new tune, "Yankee Doodle Dandy." The cheers grew louder. And a moment later the officers saw a sight none of them ever forgot.

Coming down the main street of camp was the field music—four fifers and two drummers. Close behind were three pairs of men, buckskin-shirted, coon-hatted. Hanging head down from a pole between each pair was a black bear. Behind the hunters was an immense crowd of soldiers, yelling at the top of their lungs.

"What in tarnation . . ." General Jackson began, then stopped.

"It's Davy Crockett, the Tennessee bear hunter," Colonel Coffee explained.

"And a good five hundred pounds of bear," said Jackson.

The parade came to a stop a few rods away from the big tent. Davy, Major Russell and the four scouts put down their burdens, then came to attention and gave what they thought was a snappy military salute to General Jackson.

The fierce eyes of Old Hickory softened, as did the lines of his usually grim mouth. He smiled.

"General," Colonel Coffee spoke up, "your army is not going to bed hungry."

Jackson chuckled. "I could do with a piece of steak myself," he said. "Crockett," he went on, "I heard of you up on the Holston. Did you kill your first bear when you were three years old?"

"No, sir. I shot at one when I was eight and missed him. I was a grown man nigh ten when I got my first bear."

Jackson threw back his head and laughed. "Let me shake your hand, Davy Crockett," he cried. "And now let's have our vittles."

And one of General Jackson's orderlies wrote that night in his diary: "Our supper was corn bread, molasses, and bear meat, this last thanks to the famous hunter David Crockett."

6

THE FIRST BATTLE

THE DELAYED SUPPLIES AT LAST BEGAN TO ARRIVE at the camp. So did hundreds of new volunteers, and a few score horses. Within little more than a week General Jackson had fifteen hundred men in his command.

Drilling started at once. Few of these men had ever served in the Regular Army. Some had drilled briefly in militia companies, but even they barely knew which foot to move first when the command "Forward, march!" was given.

General Jackson was in a hurry to start action against the Creeks, or, as some called them, the Redsticks. Almost every day runners came in to report fresh attacks. Settlers were killed, their womenfolk and children either killed or taken away as captives. Homes were burned.

Jackson called Colonel Coffee. "We can wait no longer to drill all these farmers," he said. "Colonel, how many *good* bushwhackers, real fighting men, can you pick out of this crew?"

The Colonel thought a moment. "Will fifty do?"

"Yes, fifty good young bushwhackers ought to do. I want you to give them the best horses in camp. You will lead the party. Find out what the Creeks are up to. Where are they the thickest?"

"Probably on the Coosa River."

"Likely so. But find out. Keep an eye on 'em. Send a runner back to me."

"I'll take Major Russell and Scout Crockett."

"But don't start a battle. Don't do any fighting unless you have to."

Jackson and Coffee talked a while longer.

Another runner came in to report a tragedy. On the Tallapoosa River three cabins had been burned. The scalped bodies of four men were smoldering in the ruins. There was no sign of women or children anywhere.

General Jackson was silent. He walked up and down in front of the tent. Then he said, "Coffee, use your own judgment. And the best of luck."

Colonel Coffee, Major Russell, Scout Crockett and forty-odd men, all mounted on good horses, made fast time getting overland to the upper Coosa River. Then followed almost a month of tracking, trying to catch up with a raiding party, chasing down what proved to be false alarms of new raids.

"We haven't seen a single Creek," Davy complained to Colonel Coffee. "What kind of war is this, anyway?"

Almost as if in answer to Crockett's complaint, a friendly Indian, a Creek, came to the white men's camp. He knew no English, but Davy knew some Creek. "He says," Crockett translated for Colonel Coffee, "there's a camp of mean Creeks no more than a day from here."

"Will he guide us?"

Davy and the Indian jabbered a while. "No, he won't. But he'll give us a good start."

"Saddle your horses," came the order, and Coffee's party, with the Indian and Crockett leading, struck out. The Indian told Davy the Creek camp was called Tallushatches. It was really a village, a sort of small headquarters. In it were women and children, and at least a hundred warriors.

The sun was high overhead when the Indian guide stopped. "I go no more," he said in Creek to Crockett. "I go away. You get to Redsticks' camp when moon come." He waved, then turned his horse and rode off to the west.

Davy and Major Russell rode on, their party behind them. It was beginning to get dark when the two men reined their animals to a stop at the same time. Both sniffed the air. "Smoke," they said in unison.

They dismounted and tethered their horses. In a few minutes Colonel Coffee and the troop came up. In hushed voices they made plans. "They're not more than a mile off," Crockett said. "Why don't I just go ahead on foot a piece and see?"

He did, and from a limb halfway up a tall pine he could see several plumes of smoke rising out of the woods far ahead. Davy took his bearings from a strip of dead timber that looked almost white in the falling darkness. Then he got down from the tree and did some more scouting.

Returning to the others, Crockett said the Creek camp was less than half a mile ahead. "It's almost all woods right up close to the spot. But the camp is in a good-sized clearing," he reported.

"Did you get close to the camp?" Coffee asked.

"Close enough to see two squaws plucking a turkey."

"Anybody hear you? What about their dogs?"

"Nobody heard me. The wind was right. Nary a dog guessed I was looking right at him."

"You ought to be court-martialed for taking such a chance," Coffee said.

"Colonel, I was just following my own rule."

"What rule?"

"Be sure you're right, then go ahead," said Davy Crockett. "What I mean, Colonel, is that I made sure I was right about that Injun camp. Now all of us can go ahead and raid it."

Dark had come. A pair of whippoorwills called to each other from somewhere in the night. A lone owl came to sit on a pine and sound his melancholy notes as Colonel Coffee's small army lay down to rest after a supper of cold water and jerked meat.

Long before daylight Crockett and the Colonel roused the party, most of whom were awake anyway. There could be no hot coffee, no warm corn bread. Jerked meat was again the fare, with a short ration of oats for the horses.

Leading the animals, the men went ahead in single file, Crockett at the front. A few stars were still out. A pale moon—"worn out," Davy called it—hung in the western sky. It was still night. Not a bird twittered as the fifty men and fifty horses advanced.

At last Davy stopped. He motioned to Coffee and Russell to come forward, then he pointed between clumps of pines. In a long narrow clearing they could see row upon row of Indian huts, but not a campfire, and not a dog. The camp was asleep.

"There she is," Crockett whispered. "We can use the horses now."

Coffee gave his orders. All were to mount where they were. He would lead half his party down the near side of the clearing. Crockett and Russell and the rest would circle the far side. When Coffee fired his pistol, both parties were to attack.

Luckily no camp dog had smelled horse or man. And none of the horses had whinnied.

Crockett and Russell's party started first, moving to the left. Then Coffee and his men moved to the right. For a few minutes all was well, then someone's horse stumbled. The rider was thrown, landing in brush that saved his neck but snapped and crackled like fire.

From the sleeping camp came the sharp bark of a dog. Then another. In an instant the surrounding forest echoed to the howling of a menagerie of dogs and horses. An instant later Crockett heard a shot. Colonel Coffee was ready to attack.

The hitherto silent camp quickly sprang into action. Drums beat wildly. Long savage yells went up as the warriors raced to mount their horses. Children cried. The squaws started wailing.

Crockett and Russell's troop turned their horses sharply toward the camp, then charged, every man yelling and with his rifle at the ready.

Coffee's men were charging from the other side. The Creeks barely had time to mount when the white men were upon them. Crockett's first shot brought down a warrior who was in the act of leaping up on his animal.

Gunfire broke out along both sides. Arrows were whistling, and Creek bullets, too, for at least half the Indians had rifles or sawed-off muskets and they were shooting. They were shooting well, too. Crockett saw one of his men fall from his horse, then another, and still another. Three men down already. Crockett loaded, and aimed. A flash lit up the pan, but the gun didn't fire. Davy turned his horse to dash back a little way while he dumped more powder into the pan. Then he aimed again. The rifle slammed, and through the thick smoke that now covered the opening, he saw a Creek fall.

In ten minutes it was all over. Creek warriors were in flight on foot and on horseback, scattering away through the trails they knew so well, leaving their women and children.

Five white men lay dead, and the clearing was fairly strewn with dead Creeks. Colonel Coffee counted no less than thirty-eight enemy dead. But there were no wounded Creeks. Six of his own men had suffered light wounds. Two more had had their skulls cracked open from tomahawk blows. The Colonel himself bound

Drums beat wildly and long savage yells went up from the Indian camp as the warriors raced to their horses.

them up as well as he could with strips torn from blankets.

The American dead were buried in a common grave, which was then piled with brush and logs and set afire. The ashes would discourage wild animals who might come to dig.

The poor wailing Indian women and children were herded together in the middle of the camp, while Crockett, the only white present who could speak their tongue, even if poorly, tried to calm them. "They expect to be butchered," he explained. "Just the way one of my own grandmothers was butchered by Creeks."

Colonel Coffee had Davy tell the women to take what they needed from their huts. He then ordered the shelters burned. And with the captives, the party, minus five of its men, moved to the Coosa River where a prison camp was started.

Meanwhile, General Jackson had drilled the raw recruits until they had some idea of military discipline. Not much, but a little. Enough to march by companies. Every man now had a gun of some kind, either musket or rifle. They were well fed. They were spoiling for action. It came sooner than the General had expected.

An Indian runner who spoke some English arrived at the main camp. He said he had a message for General Jackson. In the commander's tent, this friendly Creek said that two hundred of his tribe and several white families were bottled up in a rude fort, Talladega, farther south. None of these Indians had taken up arms. But near the fort was a band of eleven hundred painted and feathered Creek warriors. Some of these were survivors of the raid by Colonel Coffee's men, and all of them were on the warpath. They had sent a message to the Creeks and whites in the fort: "If you don't come and join us against the whites, we will take the fort and spare nobody."

The messenger to Jackson had managed to get out of the fort unseen and make his way past the surrounding Indians.

Old Hickory lost no time. Bugles sounded, drums beat. Men hurried to form companies. All was bustle and excitement when Colonel Coffee, together with Major Russell, Crockett, and their men hove in.

Coffee hastened to the General's tent. "Tarnation, but I'm glad you came, Coffee," Old Hickory said. After explaining matters he sent for Russell and Crockett. "We start for

Fort Talladega within the hour," he told them. "Coffee will take charge of a regiment in the main troops with me. I want you, Russell, and you, Crockett, to take your brave fellows ahead. Scout the lay of the land around Talladega. Then come back to meet me. We'll be moving slow enough at best. Take your horses. Fly! Fly!"

"Good luck, boys," Colonel Coffee told them, then he smiled. "Be sure you are right, Davy, then go ahead."

Major Russell's detail enjoyed a thumping good meal before they took off out of the bedlam and seeming confusion of an army preparing to move. By nightfall, they went into camp a good six miles ahead of the main force. They were up with the birds next morning, hurrying on south. By sundown they had come close enough to hear the cries and whoops of the more than one thousand Creeks who were demanding that the two hundred people within the inclosure come and join them—or else.

Crockett and Russell crept forward. The fort wasn't the stout protection the name implied. It was simply a rather wobbly-looking oblong stockade. The huge band of Creeks could take it without trouble; but they preferred the others to join them without a battle. Crockett could hear the taunts going back and forth.

"Major," he whispered, "those poor devils just don't dare to join the other Creeks. They don't trust their word any more than I would."

"What are they shouting about?"

"The bucks outside are telling how bad it's going to be if the fort Indians don't come out tomorrow," Crockett interpreted.

"What time tomorrow?" Major Russell asked.

"I don't know."

"Jackson can't get here much before noon, if then."

"Major, we've got to save those fellows in the fort. They're on our side."

"I know, Davy, but how are we going to save them?"

"I'm going back on the trail. Now. I'm going to find the General. I'm going to tell him there soon won't be any fort."

"The army must be six miles back. Maybe more."

"Sure, I know that. I'll find 'em. I'll get some of 'em here to help us by daylight."

The two men returned to where their men were camped. Davy mounted his horse, and disappeared in the dark.

7

THE FIGHT AT TALLADEGA

THE MOON WAS UP. THE WAY LOOKED CLEAR. ANY-
how, Davy had to take the chance that no
Creeks were posted along the trail. He rode
like the wind through the trees. In less than
an hour he forded a small creek and, though
he hadn't seen any sign of Jackson's camp, he
felt sure he was almost there.

"Halt!" The command seemed to come from high above the ground in a big hickory tree. Davy reined up his horse.

"Come near," said the voice. Davy walked his horse to the base of the tree. "Who are you?"

"Davy Crockett with a message for General Jackson."

"You got the password?"

"No. But I've got to see the General."

Two armed men dropped out of the thick leaves of the hickory and landed on their feet. They peered closely. Then one of them said, "Sure enough. It's Davy Crockett."

"Pass, friend." The other guard directed him toward Jackson's tent.

Davy slapped his horse. In another few minutes he was telling the General about the crisis at Fort Talladega. In another moment Old Hickory was snapping out orders. But no bugles were blown; there was no sound of drums. Jackson's aides quickly roused Captain Evans and Captain Hammond.

It was all done with the marvelous speed that was to make General Jackson the most noted commander of his time. Less than twenty minutes from the time Crockett entered Old

Hickory's tent, five hundred mounted men under Evans and Hammond were following Scout Crockett in the direction of Fort Talladega. The moon had faded now, the stars were gone, and sunrise was to find the troops still on the move. But they were moving fast for so large a body of soldiers in wooded country.

Major Russell and his men were waiting a little way from the fort. "Those Creeks know something is up," the Major said. "Some of their scouts were out all night. They spotted our camp, too."

The Major outlined his plan for battle. With his own company, he would ride boldly up to the fort. This would bring on an attack by the enemy Creeks. Russell and his men would quit their horses and enter the fort from where they could shoot at the attackers.

"Both Evans' and Hammond's men will follow Crockett. He knows the ground. He will tell you when to split up. You will divide and circle the fort." The grizzled old Major smiled. "What happens then," he said, "will depend on what the Redsticks do." He waved them away, mounted, and called to his own company to follow him. A bright sun broke through the early morning haze.

Davy Crockett watched the brave Major who chose the most dangerous spot. "No man's got more courage than he has," Davy remarked to the two captains.

Out into the clearing around the fort Major Russell led his men, their horses at a walk, as though on parade. "Look at him," said Davy. "Cool as a hog on ice."

Crockett turned to the two captains. "Let's go," he said, and started riding with Evans and Hammond at his side. Five hundred riflemen urged their horses ahead.

No sign of the enemy horde could be seen as Russell moved directly toward the fort. The top of the fort, however, was lined with copper faces, and these friendly Creeks were shouting at Major Russell and his company. They were trying to warn him, but neither the Major nor his men understood one word of all the shouting.

Crockett understood the warnings. The excited Indians were trying to make Russell understand that the enemy was concealed in thick bushes along a creek on the edge of the clearing. They yelled and gestured, telling Russell he was riding into a trap.

Russell rode on. He knew the enemy was

near. He knew they would attack when ready. He waved to the Indians on the fort.

Finally, they could stand it no longer. Two desperate Creeks leaped down from the stockade and ran headlong toward the Major, grasping his horse by the bridle in an effort to halt this slow march into a deadly trap.

At that instant the entire line of woods along the little stream seemed to vomit fire with a mighty slam that shook the ground. A vast cloud of smoke billowed over the clearing. Two of Russell's brave men toppled from their horses. Two more jumped from their mounts that had been hit.

Then, as the Major and his men leaped from their horses, the Creek army gave its war cry —a high, long screech—and came charging out of the bushes on horseback.

Russell and his men, leaving their own mounts, picked up the two wounded soldiers and hastened inside the fort, while arrows and bullets thudded into the logs. But one of the friendly Indians who had risked their lives to stop Russell fell with a long arrow through the neck.

Just as the mass of Creeks came out of the bushes, Hammond's company, with Hammond and Crockett leading, caught them from the rear. It was a total surprise. The Creeks panicked. They rode like demons around one side of the fort, thinking to escape. But they rode plumb into the rifles of Captain Evans' company and began falling right and left, horses and men together.

The entire clearing turned into a battlefield. Major Russell's men, shooting from over the stockade, picked off a Creek with almost every shot. The Creeks had no time to load again. They fought with tomahawks, and bravely.

The battle now turned into hand-to-hand combat. Crockett was trying to reload his rifle when two big Creeks attacked him with their war hatchets. Davy's gun was of no use now. He dropped it, drew his pistol and fired. He missed, and the two warriors were upon him. Using the heavy pistol as a club, he felled one Creek with a blow on the head. The other stumbled. Crockett leaped upon him, this time with his bowie knife drawn. . . .

The battle was over. It had been slaughter. Creeks lay dead all over the field. Horses, too. Seventeen white men had fallen. Six more were wounded.

In the afternoon, General Jackson arrived

ahead of his force. Major Russell reported to him that four hundred and thirty Creeks had been killed around the fort. He estimated that perhaps eight hundred others had escaped during the battle.

General Jackson was not happy to learn that so many of the enemy had escaped. He seemed to think that five hundred of his volunteers and militia should have killed every Creek at Talladega. He decided to hold his entire army at the fort for a few days, sending scouts out to see what the Creeks planned to do next.

Although Jackson didn't know it, many in his army had decided it was time for a furlough. Among these was Crockett who, like most other volunteers, had enlisted for sixty days. The time was long since past.

These men asked their officers for permission to return home for a few days. Many of them needed fresh horses and new clothing, neither of which the army could supply. All of them wanted, naturally enough, to see if their families were well. Then, too, harvest time was coming on, and many wanted to make sure there were provisions at home for the winter.

Old Hickory was short and sharp with the officers who spoke for the men. "No," he said.

"Nary a man can go now, sixty days or no sixty days."

Davy Crockett and these other frontiersmen knew nothing of military law. They felt they were entitled to a furlough, and were only being polite in troubling to ask permission. Few if any of them had any intention of deserting. But when Jackson refused, they decided to go anyway.

In the face of Old Hickory's well-known temper, this was a bold decision to make. Davy Crockett was one of the several score men who quietly got on their horses to ride out of camp by way of the bridge that had been built for the supply wagons and artillery. They found the bridge posted with guards, one of whom stood by the breech of a cannon.

"You can't cross here," said a militia officer in command of the bridge.

Crockett and the others could have forded the creek elsewhere, but that wasn't the way they wanted to leave on a furlough. After all, they were not deserting.

Davy spoke up. "I'm leaving this camp in style," he said, "and it's not stylish to swim your hoss." With that, he unslung his rifle and

uncorked his powder horn. He raised the pan
and filled it. Then he screwed the flint tight.

Crockett's idea caught on. Every man in the
group did the same. The guards on the bridge
cocked their guns. Crockett cocked his. There
was a long tense moment broken only by the
sound of the cocking of many rifles.

"Now, mister guard," Davy called out. "If
you'll just stand aside I'll cross this bridge and
be on my way." He nudged his horse. So did
the others. Out of Camp Talladega rode a long
line of riflemen who planned to have a furlough
before they did any more hunting of Creek enemies. No shot was fired.

There is no record of what Old Hickory said
when the news came to him. Doubtless he knew
the ways of frontiersmen well enough to let the
matter drop.

Davy's furlough was brief. He found Polly
and the children "in good smart health." He
hired a couple of young boys to help with the
corn harvest. He traded his worn horse for a
fresh one. Polly made him a fine new buckskin
shirt. He was ready now for more fighting. At
Winchester he met a dozen or so furlough-men
who were prepared to leave. Word had come

from General Jackson that they were to rejoin the main army at a new camp on the Tennessee River near Muscle Shoals.

When they arrived at camp, the returning volunteers found that an expedition was about to leave for the Tallapoosa River. Major Russell's company of scouts was to go, along with several companies of mounted riflemen. In command of the entire force under General Jackson was Colonel William Carroll, a gallant and brilliant officer who was later to become one of the greatest governors Tennessee ever had.

Crockett noted that though many of the troops were green and had not been under fire, they were better drilled than before. They were also better equipped. Jackson's artillery, which had totaled only two guns when Davy went on furlough, boasted ten cannon as it rumbled out of camp.

"We got considerable of an army now," Davy remarked to Major Russell.

The old Major was not too enthusiastic. "Yes," he said, "we've got more men and horses and food. We even got cannon. We have more officers. Maybe we'll fight better. But I don't know. Too many of our men have never been shot at. Being shot at is what turns a farmer into a fighting soldier."

Davy looked at the old Indian fighter, a veteran of battles against Cherokees, Choctaws, Chickasaws and Creeks. His face was scarred from a tomahawk blow. One arm was stiff from an old wound. But his eyes, peering out from under frosted brows, were clear. So too, as Davy knew, was his mind. As for fear, Russell did not know it, any more than Davy Crockett did.

"He's the greatest Injun fighter I ever see," Davy thought as they rode away for the Tallapoosa.

8

BLOOD ON THE TALLAPOOSA

THE MARCH FROM THE TENNESSEE TO THE TALLA-
poosa was made without event. Indian signs
were thick, and now and again the men of
Major Russell's company got a fleeting glimpse
of a Creek scout. But there hadn't been a brush
with the enemy until after Jackson established

camp and sent several groups of scouts out to learn what the Indians were up to.

Crockett was, as usual, with Major Russell's band of tough lads. The first night away from the army, they camped in woods with guards posted in the dark beyond the light of their campfires. Other guards were concealed high in trees around about.

It was still pitch dark when the sleeping men were aroused by a shot. One of the tree guards had fired the warning. The men on the ground hastily tossed dry brush onto the embers of the fires, then slipped into the dark. The flames leaped high. The men hoped the Indians would rush into the firelight to attack.

They did not. They began shooting into the trees to get the scouts perched there. Crockett and the others watched the flashes of the Indian guns, returning the fire. If any of these shots found a mark, no one knew. It was Indian custom to carry away their dead if possible, and no dead Indians were found when daylight came. But four of Russell's guards had fallen dead from their posts in the trees.

It hadn't been much of a battle but the Creeks had all the best of it.

Russell's scouts ranged for several miles during another two days, then returned to Jackson and the main army to report that the enemy seemed to have gathered in force near a fine fording place on the Tallapoosa.

Jackson called his officers for a council of war. Crockett was asked to attend with Major Russell, and heard the plans outlined by Old Hickory and his orders to his chief officer, Colonel Carroll.

"The Redsticks have it all figured out," the General said. "They are sure we will ford the river there. They know it's the best ford in twenty miles.

"Nigh the ford is a narrow gorge. I warrant you the place is filled with Creeks this minute. Probably eight hundred. Likely a thousand. It's an ambush.

"But, gentlemen," he went on, "we refuse to be ambushed. We will march downriver and ford it five miles below. It's not so good a ford, but the enemy is not watching it. And when once we are over, we will be in a fine position to come up the other side and attack their hide-out with artillery."

The General turned to Colonel Carroll. "Sir,"

he said, "how many fifers and drummers do we have?"

"Six fifers, sir, and three drummers."

"Well, leave 'em all here. Leave also a hundred or so soldiers. As noisy soldiers as you've got. When we march, and after we have gone, I want this camp ground to sound as though a thousand men were still here."

"What about leaving a few horses, too?"

"Mules will be better than horses," said the General. "They'll make more noise."

"General," spoke up Scout Crockett, "there's one drummer boy here's got a right fine jackass that will make more noise, and sweet, too, than a dozen mules."

Old Hickory laughed. "Fine! Fine! Stake him in the middle of camp, then put a bushel of oats just out of his reach."

There was more talk about details of the march, then the war council broke up.

At four o'clock next morning, the first company struck out downriver, followed at ten minute intervals by others. By six, the entire army was on the move. That is, except for those who were to remain to give life to the camp ground.

Instead of scouting ahead, as was their usual custom, the men of Major Russell's company were to be the rear guard. It was the place of honor. In case the Creeks discovered the army was not fording the river near the ambush gorge, they would surely try to attack Jackson from the rear. If they did, they would find Russell's hard-bitten men there, including Davy Crockett.

All went well at first. The army moved in good order down the west bank of the Tallapoosa. The all but deserted camp ground continued to *sound* as if all the white troops in Mississippi Territory were assembled there. The fifers and drummers played a rousing tune. The sharp blows of axes echoed as men pretended to chop trees for fuel. Now and then a man dropped the iron lid back on an iron kettle. Half a dozen soldiers struck up a favorite chorus:

We're on our way to Baltimore,
With two behind and two before,
Around, around, around we go,
Where oats, beans and barley grow.

The drums began again, and the fifes squealed high and clear. The ax men resumed chopping. And the make-believe cook dropped the iron lid a few times on the iron kettle. Then, in the midst of these noises, there came a sound like nothing else on earth—the air-shattering braying of the drummer boy's donkey. There he stood, this small animal, tethered to a stake, and just beyond his reach was the big basket heaped with oats. He brayed and brayed and brayed.

The army of Indians, hidden away in the nearby gorge, could hear the many sounds from the soldiers' camp ground. They remained in ambush, certain the troops would soon begin to arrive at the fording place. They would butcher the soldiers there, company by company, man by man.

But two young Creeks, curious to know what sort of animal was making that unearthly noise, decided to find out. Without asking their elders' permission they slipped away from the hideout, then climbed a tree from the top branches of which they could look down into the white men's camping ground.

These two boys were astonished to see that the terrible noise was coming from a small animal. They were bright boys, too, and as soon as they recovered from their surprise, they got down from their perch and ran as fast as they could to their own camp in the gorge. Here they told their elders that the soldiers' camp was almost bare. Only a few men remained.

The Creek chiefs acted quickly and silently. There were no war drums, there was no yelling. The warriors were ready, daubed with paint. Running for their horses, they mounted and tore out of the narrow gorge in almost military order. A hundred, two hundred, five hundred—anyone watching that day could have seen more than nine hundred warriors come pounding out of the hideaway.

Time was too precious to stop to attack the few soldiers left in the old camp. The Creeks passed it on a dead run. They were still on a dead run when they came in sight of Jackson's rear guard.

Jackson's rear guard, which was Major Russell's company, was in the worst possible position when its last man heard the pounding of the pursuing horsemen. They were in midstream, some up to their waists in water, wading, others swimming their animals in deeper places.

"Major, they're coming!" cried Davy Crockett. He reined his horse hard. The animal struggled bravely to wheel in the water and face the rear.

On came the savages, howling now, sure of victory. A cloud of arrows descended on the men in the river. The water splashed from bullets.

Major Russell wheeled his horse the instant Crockett shouted. He cried to his men to follow him. He pushed his mount toward the bank that was now a-crawl with hundreds of Creeks. The horses of the scouts did their best, wallowing, splashing, neighing, the deep water and fairly swift current hampering every move.

Jackson's artillery had just crossed the stream when the attack came. The cannon were moving up the far bank, and the men and horses made fine targets for the Creeks. They began picking off the gunners and their animals.

Just ahead of the artillery were two companies of new militia, raw troops unused to arrows or bullets. Instead of standing and shooting at the enemy across the stream, they broke and fled back into the timber and bushes.

One after the other, the artillerymen fell under the fire from the mass of Creeks. And

On came the Indians, howling now, sure of victory.

there the little brass cannons stood, useless.

Russell's small company was now the only thing that could prevent an almost certain slaughter of much of Jackson's army. With its last man, Crockett, now in front, and the Major by his side, these ninety-odd men rode directly into the middle of the swarming Creeks on the bank.

One scout fell here, another there, but their comrades moved steadily forward to the shore, out of the water, and straight up the bank, firing as they went. It was as magnificent as any charge in the long history of cavalry— this advance of backwoodsmen who knew nothing of war but plenty about fighting.

The scouts and the Creeks were now too close for arrows and bullets. The scouts met the tomahawks with clubbed rifles and long knives. And they kept moving forward. It was savage work. The Indians began to give way in the face of these coonskin-hatted demons.

Over on the far shore, Colonel Carroll was performing gallantly, bringing up men to replace the green troops who had broken at the first attack and had run away. He paused a moment to slap an officer who was hiding, then took his stand by the cannon that had no men to serve them, directing the rifle fire of the men he had brought up to cover the heroic charge of Russell's scouts. Arrows tore the Colonel's shirt. A bullet went through his hat. He paid no heed.

The fire from Colonel Carroll's troops took effect on the Creeks massed along the bank. Russell's scouts were now up the bank, riding into the enemy, their rifles swinging like clubs, their hunting knives flashing. Crockett rose up in his stirrups and took a mighty swing at a big tall Indian who seemed to be a chief. The blow struck. The chief fell, his skull cracked open.

"Lay on, boys! Make it hot!" Major Russell yelled to his men, laying about with his long sword like a windmill.

The Creeks broke at last, as Russell, Crockett and other scouts pushed into their ranks. They didn't run yet, but they gave way, dividing in the middle where the scouts fought ahead.

From across the river came a new yelling. General Jackson had returned from the head of the column. With the help of Colonel Carroll and a few soldiers, the cannon were turned about and powder was poured down their brass mouths, while Old Hickory himself snatched a ramrod and drove the charge home. In another moment, the little guns fairly leaped off the ground, belching fire and smoke. A hail of common musket bullets spattered into the Creeks like grapeshot.

Few of these Indians had ever seen a cannon in action. Fewer still had been under cannon fire. On top of Russell's bold charge, it was too much. The Creek army went to pieces.

The soldiers Colonel Carroll had brought up started to ford the river, while Russell, Crockett and company took after the fleeing Indians, chasing them up the trail, scattering others into the woods. What had started so dangerously for the troops had been turned into a Creek rout.

Old Hickory knew well enough how it had happened that way. In his dry, short manner he gave credit to Major Russell's scouts. "They exceeded my expectations," he said. "I could always have sure reliance on those men."

Long after the battle, Crockett spoke of it

as the tightest place the army was in during all the war. "If it hadn't been for Colonel Carroll," he said, "we should have been genteelly licked that time, for we were in a devil of a fix, part on one side of the creek, part on the other, the Indians all the time pouring in on us as hot as fresh mustard on a sore shin."

9

LIFE IN THE SHAKES

WITH THE ENEMY NOW SCATTERED, THE END OF
the war against the Creeks was not far off. One
more battle, plus many smaller affrays, and
the Indians were ready to ask for peace.

Now we come to a mystery. Davy Crockett
was not at the final battle at Horseshoe Bend.
He was not present when General Jackson

and the Creek chiefs signed the treaty of
peace. It is likely that Jackson sent him on
some secret mission for the army of which he
did not then or later feel at liberty to speak.

In any case, he suddenly turned up again in
Alabama, serving still with old Major Russell.
Russell's company had been detailed by Jackson to run down the many small bands of
Creeks who refused to abide by the treaty.
They continued to rove widely, hiding much
of the time, yet now and then attacking a
settler's cabin, burning, killing, taking women
and children captives.

Russell and his men chased Creeks over
much of what is now southern Alabama, and
in Georgia and Florida. Crockett did not enjoy
this campaign. He thought that the United
States, through General Jackson, had forced
an unfair peace on the Indians, compelling
them to give up their hunting grounds. He
pitied them.

It was one of Davy's boyhood friends,
George Mayfield, who had helped him to understand the plight of the American Indian.
Mayfield had been reared by Creeks. He
acted as General Jackson's interpreter at the
peace treaty. Though two of Davy's grand-

parents had been killed by Indians, and he himself had killed many a Creek, he had come to change his mind about matters. From this time on, Davy Crockett was no longer a foe of the red man. He was a friend.

When Major Russell's company was at last released from duty, Scout Crockett went home with an honorable discharge from the army. "I never," he said, "liked this business with the Indians. I'm glad I'm done with war matters."

At home again, he found that the boys, John and William, were growing tall and strong; and the little girl, Polly, was as pretty as could be. Mother Polly, however, was far from well, and soon she died. Davy buried her himself, and over her grave placed a huge limestone boulder.

The cabin now seemed desolate. For a time one of Davy's brothers and his wife helped care for the youngsters.

The nearest cabin was that of Mrs. Elizabeth Patton. Her husband, whom Davy had known well, had been killed in the Creek War. The widow was left with two youngsters, a boy and a girl.

Mrs. Patton soon became Mrs. David Crockett, a wonderful mother for the five children. Everything was fine now—except the hunting. Davy complained endlessly. There were few bears, few turkeys, almost no possums. Raccoons were as scarce, said Davy, as elephants.

The Crocketts moved still farther west and took a claim on land in a region so wild that no sort of government had been set up. The other settlers were glad to welcome the Crocketts. They had been planning to form a regiment of militia and now they had among them one of the most famous army scouts in all Tennessee. To command the regiment they selected Davy as colonel. Now that they had an army, the settlers felt they should have a court. They elected Davy judge.

Colonel Crockett was quite able to command a group of soldiers; but Judge Crockett knew nothing of law books. He had trouble enough to write his name and to read. Davy went seriously to work to improve both his reading and writing. Writing warrants, and making a record of his judgments, provided a lot of practice. He gave much time to it, and pretty soon began to inscribe a motto at the end of his documents: "Be sure you're right, then go ahead." That motto became famous.

With hunting so poor, Davy got to be quite a businessman. He dammed the creek by his cabin, and set up a water wheel to turn grindstones. This gristmill was the first of its kind in the neighborhood. Settlers came for miles to have their corn and buckwheat made into meal and flour.

When a county government was established, Crockett was asked to run for the office of representative in the Tennessee legislature. He was elected, and always liked to say he won votes simply because he let his opponents make all the long speeches. "Then," he said, "when the people were all tired out from talk, I'd tell them a story or two. They liked my stories. That's why they elected me."

While Davy was away at a session of the legislature a freshet in the creek took out his dam and washed the gristmill downstream. "Never mind, Davy," said his wife. "We'll sell everything to pay our debts and then move on."

Davy was tickled. "That's just the kind of talk I like to hear," he said. "Anyhow, this part of the country is getting too filled up."

The part of the country into which the Crocketts moved this time was wild enough for anybody. This was the region along the

Obion River in western Tennessee which flowed into the Mississippi. The nearest cabin to Davy's was seven miles distant. The next nearest was fifteen miles away.

This pleased Davy well enough, but even better was the game. Old hunter that he was, he had never seen the like. Bears were plentiful. On the river and in the lakes were beaver, mink, and otter. Wild geese came in vast flocks. Here also were the great snapping turtles with huge heads and sides of scaly armor that were to become famous in Tennessee legend.

One reason why there were so few settlers was a series of earthquakes which began in 1811, continued most of that year, and came again and again for many years thereafter. The first of the quakes had been so violent that the current of the Mississippi River itself had flowed for a time upstream. A smaller river had been turned into a long lake. Other lakes had sunk out of sight into the earth.

Here and there gigantic canebrakes, thirty feet high, had grown up along the streams. They were so thick that hunters had to cut their path through the dense canes with knives. Not long after the first big quake, a hurricane struck the region, blowing down big gum trees and hickories, stacking the canebrakes into piles of jackstraws. Both bears and cougars haunted these places.

The entire region was known as The Shakes, and here on a fork of the Obion River, in 1822, Davy Crockett and his wife, together with five children, established their home in what is now called Gibson County. It was here that Davy, at least, had perhaps the happiest years of his life.

The boys were big enough to hunt now. They dressed like their father, in long buckskin shirts, coonskin caps with the tails hanging and moccasins on their feet. Each had a rifle and powder horn.

As for the dogs, Old Whirlwind, now aged, was too lame to hunt any longer, but Soundwell, Deathmaul, and Grim were still ready to tree a coon or a cougar; and the younger Crockett hounds, such as Tiger, Growler, and Thunderbolt, had become seasoned hunters.

Davy taught his boys how to set snares and make deadfalls to take fur-bearing animals.

He brought up his children to know and respect the Indian families who lived in The Shakes, mostly Choctaws and Chickasaws. "Best hunting neighbors in the world," Davy called them. The Crocketts and Indian neighbors often exchanged provisions and supplies.

When his children asked questions, Davy never let them go answerless even when he made up the answers on the spot. He told Robbie that the possum had no fur on his tail because of his vanity. Once upon a time, it seems, possums did have furry tails, but they were not content. They wanted rings around their tails, like the raccoons. Somebody came along and told the possums they could make rings by singeing their tails all around. They tried it, and burned all the fur off their tails. The fur never grew back.

Why did possums always have grins on their faces? Easy. Long ago a possum was walking through the woods and saw what looked like a nice sweet plum on the ground. He started to eat it. But it wasn't a plum. It was a bitter oak acorn. It puckered up the possum's mouth terribly, setting his face in a grin. Possums have been grinning ever since.

Davy felt that his boys should be toughened to stand any kind of weather, and to sleep anywhere. One time when young Robbie and William were out hunting with their father, a blizzard came up. They had had to camp in the snow. Robbie thought he'd show his father how tough his son was. He made a large snowball, then lay down to sleep with his head on the snow pillow.

Sometime in the night, Robbie was roughly awakened. His father had got up to add wood to the campfire and, seeing the snow pillow, had kicked it out from beneath the boy's head. "Sissy stuff," he muttered. "I won't have any boy of mine sleeping thataway."

Davy Crockett was becoming known all over the United States as the mighty bear hunter of Tennessee. Strangers going down the Mississippi often stopped off in order to see the man of whom so many stories were told.

Davy was always glad to see them. "Light down, stranger," he'd say, then offer the hospitality of his house and table. And they would talk. Crockett was never without words. He told stories, sometimes true, often made up, of the marvels of hunting to be found in The Shakes.

"Alligators?" he said when a party of three strangers brought up the subject. "Why, they do get pretty thick around here come spring when the lakes are full. About daybreak I can hear 'em roaring like a herd of bulls. But I don't hunt 'gators. I snare one now and then.

"Last spring I got my rope over one exactly thirty-one foot long. Tamed him, I did. Now every summer he comes up beside the cabin and we use him for a bench. Mighty handy, too."

Stories like this circulated far. When some bill or other was being debated in the legislature, Representative Crockett usually had something to say; and he often said it with a story—a sort of fable.

Coming as he did from the wildest and, so some said, the toughest backwoods district in the state, Davy delighted in living up to its reputation. He said he didn't mind being called almost any sort of name except "gentleman." That made him really angry.

Newspapers here and there began to print little items about Colonel Davy Crockett of West Tennessee, the champion bear hunter and storyteller of the United States. He reveled in it.

One day two professional politicians rode horseback into The Shakes to call on Colonel Crockett. He didn't know who they were, but thought they had probably come to ask him to take them on a bear hunt. He had done as much for other strangers time and time again.

But these men had an idea. They suggested that Colonel Crockett become a candidate for Congress from the Western District of Tennessee.

If they thought Davy would be impressed beyond words, they were mistaken. Davy took the suggestion in his stride. "Maybe I'll try it some day," he said. "But right now I've got me a big job in the stave business. That'll waste time enough when I ought to be hunting bear. Bears are good and fat this season. I hate to miss my hunt. You can see I'm pretty busy. Why don't you come around again, in a year or so? I might like that Congress job first-rate."

10

DOWN THE BIG RIVER

THE STAVE BUSINESS DAVY MENTIONED TO THE politicians had to do with pipes for carrying water. Iron for this purpose had not yet come widely into use. Pipes were made by boring holes through logs from end to end, or constructed of wooden staves bound together with hoops.

Davy had been prompted into this venture because a sudden drop in the price of furs had reduced his income almost to nothing. He set a crew of men to felling trees along the Obion River and making the wood into long staves. He had another gang building two big flatboats. No less than 30,000 staves were packed snugly into the boats.

The voyage was to be down the Obion to the Mississippi, then down the big river to New Orleans. Davy himself had never piloted anything larger than a canoe. His men were as much landlubbers as he. So, to take charge of the two craft he hired a man who claimed to be one of the top pilots of the Mississippi. He called himself Captain Whale.

With men at the long sweeps of each craft, Captain Whale on deck of the leading boat and Davy on the other, the lines were cast off. All went well enough down the Obion. Then they floated out into the broad stream called the Father of Waters—and things began to happen.

The river did not look swift to the eye; it looked calm and rather lazy-like. But within a few minutes, Davy and all his men felt their coonskin caps rise. Even as they watched they saw a big long drifting log sucked down almost out of sight in a sudden whirlpool, then shoot straight up until twenty feet of it was in the air. It stayed suspended there a moment, dripping, then fell back into a fury of thrashing water.

Davy and his crew stood wide-eyed on the boat decks. "Did you see that, Davy?" one of the men asked.

"I sure did, and that log's no toothpick, either."

"She'll weigh two ton."

Davy looked ahead down the wide, wide river. Here and there he could see snags of trees standing firm in the current ready to wreck any craft. And there were "sawyers," too. These were whole trees with one end fast in the river bottom, while the rest floated near the surface, the limbs bobbing up and down. They could catch and hold large craft as in a vise.

Just then the boat Davy was riding stopped with a jolt that shivered her timbers and threw two of the crew flat to the deck. She had hit a rugged snag.

"Hang onto your teeth, boys," Davy cried.

The craft swung around, then started down-

river with her stern first. Davy leaped to one
of the sweeps. "To the oars, men," he shouted.
By the time they had the boat turned again,
the other boat, with Captain Whale at the
main sweep, had hit something. She was spinning in the current like a top gone wild.

"What kind of a pilot have we got?" Davy
complained.

"I don't think he knows any more than we
do about the river," said one of the crew.

"And we," said Davy, "don't know enough
to stay on shore where we belong."

For the next few hours the voyage was
made mainly from one snag to another, then
from one sawyer to another sawyer. The current grew faster. Night was coming on. Davy
shouted across the water to Captain Whale,
asking when he planned to tie up for the night.
"Pretty soon," came the answer.

Yet on went the boats, swirling, bumping.
Davy shouted again. "Pretty soon," said Captain Whale.

And pretty soon, too, darkness had fallen
over the river. Davy managed to get his boat
abreast of Captain Whale's. "Take us ashore,"
he ordered.

"I can't. Current's too fast."

"Were you ever a pilot on this river?" Davy cried.

"No, but I was an assistant pilot."

Davy Crockett wasn't given to swearing, but he gave the man a good tongue lashing.

On went the two boats in the dark. Captain Whale's boat barely missed a long raft of timber with bright flares burning along its rear end. The raft was already tied up for the night on the east bank. A man on the raft swung a lantern and shouted, "Why don't you tie up, you fool?"

Captain Whale couldn't tie up because he did not know how to bring his boat to land. Davy had given him a chance, several chances. Now he was certain that his pilot was a complete fake. Something must be done.

"Boys, help me get this ship nigh Captain Whale," Davy told his crew. "I'm going to board her like a pirate and take charge. I can't know less than he does."

Lurching, turning, bumping, the two boats continued their dangerous voyage. Davy's men were working like beavers on the sweep and oars, getting their craft near to Captain Whale's. The moon had now risen clear and strong. Davy stood in the bow of his craft, tense, watching the gulf of pounding current between the two boats narrow.

"One more heave, boys," he shouted. Then he leaped like a panther over the water and landed on the other boat. Captain Whale started to speak. Davy felled him with one blow.

"Give us a hand," Davy cried. "Let's tie our navy together."

Swishing through the air came ropes from the other boat, and in another minute the two craft were lashed together. Captain Whale was sitting up now, rubbing his jaw.

"I've not got breath to tell you what I think of fake pilots, Captain Whale," Davy said. "But *I'm* captain now. You can stay right where you are."

The double-boat churned on. With two stout men on each of the two sweeps, the monster kept her nose where it belonged, which was ahead.

Davy cheered his crews. "If we're going to be wrecked," he called out, "let's wreck the whole shebang together."

Lights twinkled in the dark along the shore. Now and again somebody hailed the strange craft. Soon they caught up with a big boat from

the Ohio and for a few minutes cruised alongside. Davy shouted to the skipper, asking ad-
vice.

"You might as well run all night," he told
Crockett. "I do it most of the time."

"But we're no sailors."

"Well, do your best. And keep out of Davy
Jones' locker."

"I'll try to. I'd rather be in Davy Crockett's
locker."

The Ohio boatman laughed. "Davy Crockett's
locker," he replied, "is likely full of bear meat."

The moon went behind a cloud. A covey of
ducks rose almost from under the two boats,
jabbering, and took off upriver. Over near the
far shore appeared a long string of lights close
to the water. Davy guessed it was another big
raft of timber going down for the New Orleans
sawmills.

The current turned swifter, almost racing.
Though neither Davy Crockett nor any of his
crew knew it, they were approaching a wild
reach of the river called the Devil's Elbow. But
soon enough they knew they were in for trouble.
Directly ahead, the wide river was split by an
island. The upper end of the island was covered house high with drift timbers, wild logs,

uprooted trees, mountains of branches and debris.

"Hard, boys, hard on the oars!" Davy was trying to be Captain Crockett. The men *worked*, sweating at the long oars. But in spite of all, the clumsy craft slowly turned and began to go sideways. In another moment it struck with a mighty crash into the hard-packed driftwood on the island.

"Every man for himself," Davy shouted.

The side of one of the boats was stove in. Water started to fill her hold. Both boats seemed to hesitate for an instant, and then, still lashed together, they reeled with a lurch that tossed all on deck into the river or into the mass of driftwood.

Davy and all hands were safe, though bruised. The boats swung away, the full force of the current hit them, and they disappeared in the dark.

The first streaks of dawn found Davy Crockett and his men, along with Captain Whale, sitting on the east shore of the island. Davy felt discouraged. His venture with staves had ended in disaster. But he hadn't lost his humor.

"Boys," he announced in the tones of a man making a speech, "boys, the people of West

Tennessee demand that I save them and save the country by running for Congress.

"I plan to get a law passed to prevent fools from going into the wood stave business. And another law providing for the hanging of fake river pilots."

A little after daylight the marooned men hailed a large boat coming downriver. A skiff was sent ashore, and the Crockett crew was taken aboard and given a ride to Memphis. Here Davy borrowed enough money from an old comrade, Major Winchester of the Creek War days, to take himself and the crew back to the Obion. He later learned that one of his boats —they had broken their lashings—had been seen some fifty miles below Memphis, partly stove-up and the cargo lost. The other was never seen again, so far as Crockett could find out.

When he saw the familiar woods of the Obion again, Davy said he wanted nothing so much as a good bear hunt. He took Old Betsy down from its pegs, and spent a happy hour cleaning and oiling the gun, while his hounds wagged and whined. They knew what was in store.

When a friend dropped in to ask him about Congress, Davy replied he would take up that matter as soon as more important business had been cared for. Swinging rifle over shoulder, his dogs yelping, the greatest bear hunter in Tennessee and the United States struck out for the wildwood of The Shakes.

11

FRIEND OF INDIANS

DAVY'S HUNT WORKED OUT ABOUT AS USUAL. IN five days he had a couple of fairly large black bears, and an elk. He also ran out of powder. This meant a trip down to the settlement. Making up a bundle of furs which his sons had caught during the previous winter, Crockett rode to the general store to get a keg of powder, some lead to make into bullets, and a length of gingham for his wife.

No cash changed hands, of course. Business was conducted according to the barter system. In other words, a customer traded furs for what he needed of store goods. When the storekeeper had gone through and counted Crockett's pile of furs, he was a little surprised to find that it consisted mostly of mink, with a few otter and half a dozen wildcat skins.

"What happened to the coons?" the merchant asked. "Aren't you getting coons any more?"

"Yes, there are still plenty of coons around my place. I reckon I got me ten skins at home."

"Why didn't you bring 'em in?"

"Tell you how it is," Davy said. "I'm fixing to run for Congress this fall. I'll need a couple of right fine coonskin caps when I get to Washington."

The merchant laughed. "You seem to be pretty sure you're going to win."

"Likely I will. I figger my opponents will beat themselves by talking too much."

After getting his store goods, Davy took a roundabout way home, stopping a while at every cabin to talk. Many of these men were veterans of the Creek War and knew Crockett for his ability as a fighting man. Davy let them know he was running for Congress in the fall campaign.

"I reckon lots of folks will think it's a joke," he said, "a bear hunter going to the Congress." It tickled Davy, too. "Those people in the towns—you know what they think of us backwoodsmen in The Shakes."

The newspapers all over Tennessee played it up:

DAVY CROCKETT, CHAMPION BEAR HUNTER,
TO RUN FOR SEAT IN CONGRESS

Editors made up stories. They quoted Crockett as saying he would start his campaign "with a few speeches tied up in an alligator hide"; that if elected he planned a bill to remove the national capital "to the banks of the Obion in West Tennessee."

Two other candidates appeared. Both were men of some wealth and experience, compared to Crockett. After a few weeks, when the campaign began to get really warm, it was arranged for all three men to speak on the same day, and from the same stump. The two profes-

sionals pretended that Crockett wasn't running. They wholly ignored him in their ap-
peals for votes. The campaign, they seemed to
think, was just between themselves.

The meeting was held on the edge of a
swamp. All the while the speeches were going
on they were accompanied by some powerful
calling of bullfrogs. When Davy got up to talk
he told a bear story or two, never so much as
mentioned his two opponents, and wound up
with a typical Crockett touch. Davy, who could
imitate any animal, said he was highly pleased
at the support he was getting in all quarters.
Then, from deep down in his throat, came a
perfect echo of the nearby frogs: "Cro-o-o-ck-
ett-tt! Cro-o-o-ck-ett-tt!" No ventriloquist ever
did better. The crowd roared—that is, all except Davy's opponents. They were quiet.

Crockett's friends in The Shakes, and
throughout much of the West Tennessee con-
gressional district, did everything possible for
their candidate. They held barbecues, squirrel
hunts, and dances, at all of which Davy appeared to tell a few stories, shake many hands,
and talk of the stirring days of the Creek War.
More important, on election day all of Crock-

ett's friends were up with the sun, going on foot or horseback from cabin to cabin, urging citizens to vote. Representative Crockett was elected by a good majority.

Representative Crockett, from West Tennessee, was a sensation in Washington where he promptly became known as the Coonskin Congressman. Nothing like him had been seen in the national capital.

A favorite story had it that when he entered a Washington hotel to get lodgings, the clerk asked who he was. "Who am I?" repeated Davy. "Why, I'm David Crockett, fresh from the backwoods, half horse, half alligator, a little touched with the snapping turtle.

"I can wade the Mississippi, leap the Ohio, ride a streak of lightning, slip without a scratch down a honey locust, whip my weight in wildcats, hug a bear too close for comfort and eat any man opposed to Jackson." (Crockett's old general was to become the seventh President of the United States in 1829.)

If the hurry and bustle of Washington was at first a little bewildering to the new congressman, he took it in his stride. He was too shrewd not to live up to the part expected of him as the Coonskin Congressman from the backwoods. He pretended ignorance of manners and customs. He said that city food did not agree with him; next time he would bring along a good big mess of salted bear meat.

During his first term, he spoke rarely in the House of Representatives, but when he did his native wit and backwoods humor held the attention of everyone. When it was known he was to address the House, the visitors' gallery never failed to be filled.

For the press, he could always be depended upon for a story, or some comment. "Members of Congress earn every penny they are paid," he told the newspapermen. "That is, if they don't go to sleep during them long speeches. I tell you it's dreadful hard work to keep awake and listen to talk that means nothing. Splitting gum logs in August is a sight easier."

At the end of his term Crockett was reelected. This time Congress was to be a battleground over the issue of public lands. In various ways, some legal, some not, speculators had got their hands on hundreds of thousands of acres of wild country. They set high prices on land that had cost them little or nothing.

Crockett belonged to the group which wanted these lands made available to settlers who wanted farms and homes.

Here was a matter about which Crockett knew a good deal. He began to speak often in debates in the House, always briefly, and with wit, but also with great force. Again and again, however, the bill he sought to introduce in Congress was set aside. And when it did come up for vote, it was defeated.

Crockett also lost another battle. This had to do with Indian lands in several states but chiefly those in Georgia. Gold had been discovered in several sections of these lands, and white adventurers swarmed in despite a federal law which prohibited them. These invaders often drove Indians from their villages by force. A few whites were killed in these clashes.

Though most of the Indian villages were more orderly than the white settlements, politicians charged them with being places of violence. The states of Florida, Georgia, Alabama, and Mississippi demanded that all Indians be removed to reservations in the far West.

President Jackson himself favored their removal. Sorely disappointed in his old hero,

In Congress Davy spoke out in defense of the Indians.

Crockett went headlong into the fight to leave the poor red men where they had lived since before Columbus came to America.

The President sponsored a bill to remove five tribes to new territory beyond the Mississippi River. All of the Tennessee delegation in Congress supported Jackson's bill except Crockett. He stood up to say that Congress was attempting to break a treaty which the tribes had signed at the end of the Creek War and which said that the Indians should remain in possession of their old hunting grounds.

"This treaty is the highest law of the land," he cried in the House. "But there are those who do not find it so. They would juggle with the rights of the Indian and fritter them away. I would rather be an old coon dog belonging to a poor man in the forest than belong to any party that will not do justice to all."

The battle went on. When it appeared that Jackson's bill would pass and become law, Crockett demanded an investigation of the lands to which it was proposed to send the Indians. He pointed out that the Creeks, the Cherokees and the other eastern tribes concerned had always lived in villages. If moved to the far West, they would be raided and killed by the roving warlike bands of Comanches, Osages, Pawnees, and Sioux. He pleaded that to move the eastern tribes there would be little less than committing mass murder upon them.

Crockett's friends warned him he had best not persist in his opposition to a bill President Jackson wanted passed. Crockett's reply became famous. "I'll wear no man's collar," he said. "Long ago I fixed on a motto—'Be sure you're right, then go ahead.' I mean to follow it no matter what the President wants."

The bill was passed. Crockett's hot opposition to it made him unpopular at home in Tennessee. Most people there did not care what happened to a few thousand Indians. The voters in his district defeated Crockett roundly when he ran for re-election.

For the next two years he became Davy Crockett the old bear hunter again. With a little farming at home to break the hunts, he ranged through The Shakes with his dogs. The bears were not so thick as they used to be. One wonders if Davy realized why, or whether he gave thought to the several hundred animals he had killed since moving to the Obion.

In any case, he got around a good deal and talked with everybody; and in 1833, though many of the same people opposed him, he was again elected to Congress.

The vacation was probably a good thing for Crockett. He was missed in the national capital where he had become something of a celebrated character. His return was a triumph. Though he was no longer a member of the militia, he was now and forever after called Colonel Davy Crockett.

Colonel Crockett and General Jackson were now political enemies. The new Whig party

Whig leaders presented Davy with a handsome rifle.

adopted Davy as one of their champions. He was banqueted. Whig newspapers printed everything he had to say, and often made up things he never said. A beautiful rifle was presented him by a group who described themselves as "The Whig Gentlemen of Philadelphia." It was a handsome gun, the stock trimmed in sterling silver, with engraved figures representing Liberty, a racoon, a deer's head, and a bear. And in silver letters, engraved near the muzzle, were the words: "Go Ahead."

Colonel Crockett made a tour of the North which added to his fame. In Philadelphia, New York and Boston he was given the key to the city, and spoke at dinners in his honor. Meanwhile, he attacked Jackson's policies in regard to public lands and removal of the eastern Indians. When chance offered in the House, he rose to say once more that the Indians were being shamefully treated.

One of Jackson's close friends, a typical Southern fire-eater of the period, took offense at something Crockett said, and sent a messenger to him with a formal challenge to a duel.

Davy, though never a man to dodge a fight, considered duels childish. "Tell him I'll meet him," he told the messenger. "Since he is the challenger, I may pick the weapons. Tell him we'll fight with bows and arrers."

All Washington laughed with Davy. The challenger was ridiculed until he left the city. Crockett pretended that the man was really afraid of him. "He knowed," said Davy, "that I am more clever with a bow and arrer than William Tell was. I used to let fly with a neat feathered arrer and take the core right out of an apple resting on the head of my young son Willie Crockett."

The newspapers played the story up as an actual fact. And when, a few days later, Davy went to see a menagerie and asked permission to get into the cage with a hyena in order "to grin the fur off his back," the press featured it as an actual happening.

Just before Congress adjourned for the summer, a new play founded on Davy Crockett and entitled "The Lion of the West" appeared. It was mostly myth, yet it added to the fame of Colonel Crockett. He was becoming a legend even while he lived.

At the last session of the House, Crockett arose to condemn once more what he termed "The Trail of Tears" which the United States was forcing the Creeks, the Cherokees and other tribes to take. "Their fair promises," he said, referring to a majority of his fellow Congressmen, "are worth about as much as a flash in a pan when you have a shot at a fat bear." With that he went home to West Tennessee.

12

COLONEL CROCKETT GOES WEST

COLONEL CROCKETT'S ROUTE HOME WAS BY STAGE-coach to Pittsburgh, Pennsylvania, where he took passage on the steamer *Hunter* to Louisville, Kentucky. News of his coming went ahead of him, for awaiting his arrival was the largest crowd that had ever been seen in the city. A band played. At the courthouse he addressed the citizens, then was taken to a hotel for an immense dinner.

Next day he continued on down the Ohio to Mills Point, Tennessee, where his son William met him. From there it was a 35-mile horseback ride to the Crockett home near the headwaters of the Obion River.

After a few days with his family, Davy struck out, not on a bear hunt but to campaign for re-election to Congress. It was going to be a tough battle for votes. His opponent was Adam Huntsman, who had lost one leg in the Creek War. He wanted to go to Congress. Long before Davy had returned home, Huntsman was riding all over West Tennessee, talking to the voters.

It is possible that Davy did not realize how much dislike his stand in favor of the Indians had created in his district. Then, too, the newspapers had used his tour of New England against him. They said Crockett had "turned Yankee." At the fall election he was defeated by a narrow margin.

It was a bitter blow. He had fought in Congress for the small landowners against the big speculators, the land sharks. He had also fought for the Creeks and Cherokees, demanding that they be permitted to remain on their tribal hunting grounds. He had lost both of those battles. Now he had lost another.

Davy Crockett was not a man to sit and moan. If Tennessee did not want him, then perhaps the new country of "The Texas," as it was called, would welcome him. Crockett was soon writing a friend: "I am on the eve of starting for The Texas. Three men and myself will make up the company. We will go through Arkansas and I want to explore The Texas before I return."

It was hardly surprising that a man as restless as Davy Crockett should have wanted to go to Texas in 1835. Things were stewing there. There was excitement, even a shooting war. And there was enough wild vacant land for a million men to get lost in.

The country we call Texas today was then a province of Mexico. In 1821 a man from Connecticut, Moses Austin, got permission from Mexico to establish a colony of American families in the province. He died soon after; but a son, Stephen Austin, moved to the colony with 300 American families. A little later be brought in 700 more people.

For several years all went well with the

American settlers. But the Mexican government was unstable. The Americans would not learn Mexican ways or speech. They had difficulty with Mexican courts and army officers. The troubles increased. Then, just before Davy Crockett left Tennessee for the West, the Americans in Texas rebelled and declared their land to be an independent republic.

They raised an army, and put in command of it General Sam Houston, a former soldier in the Creek War who had also served as governor of Tennessee. Houston and Stephen Austin issued an appeal that was printed in newspapers in all parts of the United States. They asked for volunteers to come to fight for the independence of the Texas republic.

Davy Crockett was on the way, alone. (What happened to the other three men he mentioned in his letter is not known.) From his home he went by boat down the Obion, then by trail to Mills Point where a big, handsome, brightly-painted steamboat took him down the Mississippi.

Davy was dressed in buckskin shirt and leggings. A new coonskin cap was on his head, the ringed tail hanging down behind. With him he carried the silver-mounted rifle that had been presented to him by his Philadelphia friends.

In the ship's company were other men dressed much the same as Crockett. There were planters, too, in quiet broadcloth, stock ties and beaver hats; and their women in furs and bombazines. There were a few soldiers in blue, probably on furlough.

The outstanding figures on board were a couple of young fellows in tight yellow trousers, waistcoats like rainbows, and ruffled white shirts with great glittering studs that may have been diamonds. Crockett knew their type. They were riverboat gamblers.

With smoke pouring from her tall stacks, the boat swept on with the current down the great stream. She passed the mouth of the White River that entered the Mississippi from Arkansas. Then came the Arkansas River, flowing wide and full. Hours later the steamer whistled for the settlement of Little Rock, capital of Arkansas Territory, soon to be a state.

Davy found a large number of people at the only tavern. He knew they were not there to greet him; nobody knew he was coming. It turned out that they had come to see a Punch and Judy puppet show. Davy attended the performance, too, and presently the tavern-keeper came to him. "Are you not Colonel Crockett?" he asked.

"At your service, sir," replied Davy.

Whereupon the tavern-keeper got busy and saw to it that a dinner was given in honor of the famous man. When asked to speak, Davy told the audience he was heading for Texas. "There's something happening down there," he said. "Something that makes me feel I should be on the ground."

Because his way from Little Rock was overland to Fulton on the Red River, Crockett's hospitable new friends supplied him with a horse, then insisted on riding in company with him for the first fifty miles of his journey. (Then as now Arkansas people were noted for their kindness to strangers.)

In Fulton Crockett began to hear a great deal of talk about Texas. At the town of Natchitoches, farther down on the Red River, a number of men had already left for the excitement. Crockett got aboard a small steamer heading for Natchitoches.

The little boat was packed with cotton and people. When Crockett went out on deck to watch the scenery glide past, he noticed a tall man wearing a purple waistcoat, the usual ruffled shirt and frock coat of the gambler, and a high white hat. On a small table in front of him were three thimbles. "He looks," Davy thought, "just right for a thimblerigger."

The tall gambler kept up a stream of talk, inviting passengers to guess under which thimble he hid a pea. It was an old game, older than playing cards, as old as dice. Davy watched as the fellow deftly picked up the thimbles one after the other, put them back on the table, then challenged any passenger to bet on which thimble concealed the little pea.

A swaggering young woodsman took up the challenge. Again and again he bet, but each time he lost. When the woodsman's money was gone, the tall gambler looked at Crockett. "Come, stranger," he called, "take a chance. It's like finding money."

Crockett stepped up to the table. The gambler talked on, meanwhile doing a good deal of shuffling and passing the pea from one thimble to another. "The eye is quicker than my hand," he said. Davy knew how the dishonest trick was worked: If the pea happened to be under the thimble chosen, the gambler, when he picked up the thimble, would grasp the pea and conceal it in the crook of his little finger. The bettor couldn't win.

"Tell you what I'll do," Davy said. "If I pick the right thimble, then you will stand treat for the crowd. If I don't pick the right thimble, then I'll stand treat."

"It's a bargain," the gambler said, then went on moving the pea and the thimbles. The instant he stopped, Davy spoke: "The pea is under the middle thimble." And before the man could make a move, Davy reached out and lifted the thimble. There was the pea.

The white-hatted man was not disturbed. "Mister," he said, "your eye's as keen as a lizard's. But I don't mind if I give you another chance."

"It would be robbery," said Davy. The crowd laughed. The gambler tried to interest others among the onlookers but there were no takers.

The little steamer wound around bend after bend until Crockett came to believe that the Red River was all that the Arkansas people claimed for it—the crookedest river on earth. Time dragged into night. But at last the boat whistled and tied up at a wharf lighted with great flares of pitch pine.

Crockett went ashore with the others, and

was directed to the tavern. To his great surprise, the first person he saw in the hotel was Thimblerig himself, his tall white hat on his knees, the thimbles in a row on top of the hat. "Come, gentlemen," he was calling. "Your eye is quicker than my hand." He appeared to be doing very well.

At daybreak next morning, Davy went out to look over the town of Natchitoches. Already up was a rugged young man who seemed to be waiting for Davy. His face was tanned the color of mahogany, and he was wearing a buckskin shirt and carrying a fine rifle.

"Are you Colonel Crockett?" he asked, then explained he had heard that the famous man was going to Texas. "I'd like for to go with you," he said.

He looked to Davy like a good man to have along in a wild country. "Young feller," Crockett told him, "I'm fixing to help the Texans. That means fighting."

"Well, I done some fighting too," said the young man. "I happen to be a bee hunter, but I'm a good shot and I can navigate the woods and the prairies. I might come in handy."

Davy liked the youth. "Let's go have some breakfast," he said. They talked, and the youth

The three horsemen headed for Texas.

told Davy he knew where they could get good horses cheap. Davy gave him some money and said to go buy a couple.

Just then Thimblerig sidled over. "Colonel," he said, "I didn't know who you were on the boat. I want to go to Texas. My friend you were with, the Bee Hunter, he told me you were going there yourself."

Davy looked at the gambler. "Are you," he asked, "good for anything except thimble-rigging?"

"Yes, sir, I am. I'm afraid of nothing. I'm a

pretty good shot. I can ride. And I am not a crook. I'm a professional gambler. I want to fight for the Texans."

The Bee Hunter came up with two horses. He spoke to Thimblerig in a familiar way. "You know this feller?" Crockett asked.

"Yes, Colonel, I've known Thimblerig for a long time. He wanted me to ask you about going to Texas. I told him he must speak for himself."

Crockett questioned Thimblerig closely. The tall man's answers seemed straight enough. Finally Davy said, yes, he could go along too, if he could get a horse.

"I've got the money and I'll buy one," the gambler said. The thimbles had paid off well at the tavern.

"Better get a rifle, too," Crockett advised him.

Early that afternoon the three horsemen rode south and west, heading for whatever adventures Texas had to offer.

13

THE LONE STAR REPUBLIC

FOLLOWING THE OLD SPANISH TRAIL TO THE Sabine River, Crockett and his companions forded the stream at a place showing signs that many horsemen were ahead of them. After another day's ride the town of Nacogdoches came into view. At almost the same moment the sound of bugles and fifes and drums came tingling on the air.

"Getting ready for independence," Colonel Crockett observed. But it was something else also. Out of the settlement at a smart canter came an imposing troop of mounted men. They swept up to within a few yards, then quickly stopped, their leader riding forward alone. His long saber flashed in a graceful salute.

"Welcome, Colonel Crockett, to the Republic of Texas!" Someone barked an order, and the hundred horsemen brought their rifles and carbines to "present arms" position.

Here was a welcome to warm the honest heart of Davy Crockett. He was as pleased as he was surprised. How had word of his coming got to this remote place? Also, how did you return a salute when you had no sword and your rifle was slung over your back?

Colonel Crockett solved the problem. He took off his coonskin cap with a quick, sweeping gesture, and bowed. "Gentlemen," he said, "greetings from the state of Tennessee!"

The troop of horsemen now fell in behind their commander who, with Crockett and his companions, led the procession back to the settlement. As they entered a cannon boomed, and a bright flag was run quickly up a tall pole. It had one red stripe and one white stripe with a single star in its field of blue.

The fife-and-drum corps resumed its blaring. Smoke floated down the street where a crowd of more than two thousand people cheered wildly. Davy Crockett felt pretty good. He had left Tennessee alone. Now he was entering the Texas country to the greeting of cannon, music, and cheers.

The Bee Hunter, who had been in Nacogdoches before, went to visit friends. Thimblerig disappeared into a tavern. Crockett was taken to military headquarters and given the latest news of the Texans' efforts to break away from Mexico.

The rallying point for volunteers, he was told, was at San Antonio de Bexar, many days' ride south and west from Nacogdoches.

"Who is in command of the volunteers?" Crockett asked.

"Colonel James Bowie."

"He's the knife-man—the Arkansas Toothpick Man." Davy referred to the famous bowie knife invented by the Colonel.

"Yes, that's Bowie. And commanding what we call our Regular Army is Colonel William Travis."

"Where's Sam Houston?" Crockett wanted to know.

"He is commander in chief. But for some weeks past he has been in north Texas arranging a treaty with the Indians there. We don't want them to gang up with the Mexicans."

"What are conditions in San Antonio?"

"We have held the town since December, when our men under Colonel Edward Burleson drove the Mexicans into the nearby fort, the Alamo, and forced them to surrender."

"I know Burleson," Crockett said. "We fought together in the Creek War. He's a good man."

"We've got as good men as you can find. Our trouble is that we don't have near enough men."

"If you're in the recruiting business," Davy said, "then why don't you take me into your army?"

His hosts were delighted. They placed in front of him a paper bearing the oath of allegiance to Texas. Davy read it through, noting that it called for support "of the provisional government or to any future government that may be declared."

Before signing he asked if it would be proper to insert the word "republican," so that the oath should read: ". . . will bear true allegiance to any future republican government." The word was added. Colonel Crockett signed. He refused a commission as colonel. He was now a private in the Texas army.

Daybreak found Crockett, Thimblerig, and the Bee Hunter many miles west of Nacogdoches, riding south and west. Their goal was San Antonio. Day after day they rode on, the prairie broad and brilliant under the biggest sky Crockett had ever seen. At night, a big moon rode the sky. The stars seemed bright and near in this thin air.

There was plenty of food for a while—prairie chickens, wild turkeys, rabbits. Near the Trinity River they stopped overnight in the cabin of an old woman. It was here that Crockett recruited two more men who said they wanted to fight the Mexicans.

These two were strange travelers who had arrived at the cabin soon after Crockett and his friends. One was a tall, raw-boned fellow, with coal-black hair and fierce black whiskers. There was a deep scar across his forehead. The backs of both hands also showed scars. He wore no hat. Instead, a bright red handkerchief was bound around his head.

The other was an old, old Indian, his face lined like ancient leather. He wasn't much given to conversation, but he hadn't been inside the cabin very long before he drew a couple of fat rabbits from a bag, to which he added a dozen or so big duck eggs. "Everybody eat," was all he said.

During the meal Crockett eyed the black-whiskered fellow, thinking how much he looked like a pirate in a book. Thus he was not much surprised when the fellow let it be known that he had sailed with Jean Lafitte. Lafitte was of course the famous adventurer and outlaw who for some years had a hide-out on the coast of Texas.

"Why don't you join us to fight in the Texas army?" Crockett asked the Pirate.

"Don't mind if I do," that worthy replied. "Me and my friend was heading west, anyways."

The conversation was still lively when the old Indian, who had been quietly smoking a stone pipe, spoke up. All he said was, "Buffalo."

Everybody listened. They could hear nothing but the wind in the long prairie grass. "What do you mean, buffalo?" asked the Pirate.

"Buffalo," repeated the red man.

The talk resumed, but within a minute it stopped. Everyone could hear a far-off rumbling, something like thunder. The ground began to tremble ever so slightly. Then it began to shake. Crockett stood up. Not far to the west a cloud of dust was rising from the prairie, and out of it were coming several large dark animals. Crockett grabbed his rifle.

"I've never seen buffalo before," he said.

On came the herd, a pounding, driving mass of black beasts, thousands of them, led by a monster of a bull, as shaggy as could be.

Crockett took careful aim and fired. The bull let go a roar, then turned partly away and charged on, the others after him. The great hunter of Tennessee had not missed. His bullet had hit the bull fair, but had doubtless come to rest in the layer of thick fat.

Davy Crockett was astonished. He had believed there wasn't an animal that could stand up after being hit with a bullet from his rifle. But here was the bull running away! Davy rammed in a new load. Then he ran to his horse, leaped on its back, and away they tore after the herd.

A half mile or so farther on, he came within shooting distance. He had to shoot while riding at a very fast pace, but this time the bullet penetrated its target. A fair-sized calf dropped out of the herd, then fell. The rest thundered on into the distance.

That night, for the first time, Crockett tasted buffalo steak. He found it good. "Better than most bear," he said.

To top off the feast that evening was some fine honey which the Bee Hunter had brought into camp. He had found a bee tree not far off, and had taken a gallon or so of the honey, having been stung only twice in the process. The meal turned out to be the last festive occasion for the five men until they reached San Antonio.

The way led on, now passing through groves of live oaks bearded with long silvery moss, then into the twisted mesquite, where hundreds of rattlesnakes sunned themselves, and lizards and Gila monsters crawled over the rocks and reminded Crockett of small alligators. For two weeks the hunting was poor. Both men and horses had to live sparingly.

They met no other travelers until the day before they were due to reach San Antonio. The Pirate was riding ahead when he saw men on horseback coming. He turned to call to Crockett. "Colonel," he said, pointing, "better look out for squalls."

Davy looked and saw fifteen or twenty horsemen riding slowly and directly toward them.

"They're Mexicans," said the Pirate.

Crockett took charge. "Spread and dismount," he told his men. They drove up, then scattered right and left to form a line with Crockett at the center. They dismounted. Each man stood behind his horse, rifle barrel resting on the animal's back.

The strange horsemen continued to approach. One of them, a big man with a red feather in his hat, shouted something. Crockett could not understand the language but he did not like the tone of voice.

"What did he say?" he asked the Pirate.

"He says to lay down our guns and surrender."

"Tell him to go jump in the lake if he can find a lake," said Crockett.

The Pirate shouted in Spanish. The red-feathered fellow shouted back.

"He says to surrender," the Pirate translated. "If we don't, he will be obliged to cut our throats."

"Tell him," cried Davy, "to make sure he's right before he goes ahead." Then he turned to his men. "Hold your fire," he muttered.

The Pirate shouted Crockett's reply. The Mexicans talked no more. They fired, all at once. The shots went wild. Bullets whistled close over the Americans' heads but neither the men nor the horses were wounded.

Crockett gave the word. "Pour it on," he said. Five rifles slammed, and from behind the clouds of smoke came shouts and a cry.

Crockett and his men loaded as fast as they could, while Davy watched the smoke blow away. "Three down," he shouted. The red-feathered man and two others lay still on the ground. Three riderless horses were bounding away. So were the surviving Mexicans. The Americans fired after them but the range was too great.

Davy was elated. "Three cheers for the Lone Star Republic!" he cried. He was more than pleased with this first skirmish with the enemy.

"Boys," he said, "this is the way to join the army in style. We're not even there yet but we fought and won a battle."

The five men rode on through the gathering dusk. In the distance they soon could see the faint outlines of the town of San Antonio, where lights were beginning to shine. As they came up to the gates of the little old mission, which was used as a fort and called The Alamo, a sentry challenged them.

"Who's there?"

"Colonel Davy Crockett and party."

"Advance and give the countersign."

Davy didn't know the countersign, but he had an answer ready anyway.

"Half-horse and half-alligator," he said, "and greased with a little forked lightning. Pizen clean through."

The sentry was alarmed. He called the guard.

"No," Davy told the corporal, "I don't know the countersign, but if you will bring Colonel Travis or Colonel Bowie I'll explain matters."

In another moment the corporal returned, a tall fair-haired man in buckskin with him. "Who are you, stranger?" the tall man asked.

"Davy Crockett of Tennessee."

The tall man came forward with a bound.

"Speak of the devil!" He grabbed Davy by the hand. "We've been looking for you all day," he said. "What happened?"

"Got off on the wrong track, Jim Bowie," Davy replied, "and we had to shoot our way back to the trail."

Leading the five men into the fort, Bowie paused a moment to shout at the top of his powerful voice: "Turn out, everybody! Turn out for Davy Crockett of Tennessee and his brave men!"

Into the parade ground, lighted all around with torches, came men by twos and in dozens, shouting, clamoring to shake hands with the celebrated Indian fighter and hunter. Their spirits were raised high now that five more soldiers had been added to their pitifully small army in the Alamo.

14

A HERO OF THE ALAMO

AS SOON AS THE NOISY WELCOMES WERE OVER, Crockett sat down with Colonel Travis and Colonel Bowie.

"Colonel Crockett," said Travis, "we are in a serious position. Scouts came in only today to report that General Santa Anna, commander in chief of the Mexican army, is marching to invade Texas with several thousand men."

"He has plenty of artillery, too," put in Bowie. "Says he will blow the Alamo into dust if we don't surrender."

"The Alamo looks like a pretty rugged place," Davy said. "You got any cannon here?"

"Yes, at least two good ones. And a fair supply of powder."

"How many men in the fort?"

"We had one hundred and twenty before you came."

"And now there are one hundred and twenty-five," Davy said. "Seems like we ought to have another couple of hundred if we are fixing to hold out against the whole Mexican army."

"True enough. We have sent messengers to Goliad where the volunteers are gathering. No word has come back."

Colonel Travis explained that some Texans felt that no attempt should be made to hold the Alamo. "But," he went on, "this is the outpost. It is our first defense against attack by the Mexicans. We know they are coming. If we can hold this fort and delay them even if only for a few days, it will give the Texas army time to get ready."

"Volunteers are collecting by the hundred

at Goliad," added Bowie. "More guns and supplies are coming it. Give 'em a week more and they can take on Santa Anna."

Crockett spoke: "And the only way to give 'em that week is for us to get real mad and hold this fort."

"That's about it," Bowie agreed.

"I'm mad already. Let's hold the Alamo."

The three men shook hands.

For the next four days the small but stoutly built fort was a scene of intense activity. The cannon were cleaned. They were loaded with care. The rifle of every man was inspected. Colonel Travis sent out a force for provisions; and ninety bushels of corn and the salted meat of twenty steers were added to the fort's supply.

The defenders were cheered on the third day by the arrival of thirty-one volunteers, all with good rifles. They brought the garrison's strength to one hundred and fifty-six men. This was the "army" that must stop and delay Santa Anna and his 3,000 troops—if Texas was to gain its independence.

The Mexican residents of San Antonio were already leaving. On the morning of February

22, 1836, guards along the top of the Alamo's walls could see the first units of the Mexican army approaching.

A day later General Santa Anna's entire force was in sight. A regiment of brightly uniformed soldiers marched into the deserted town. The General set up his headquarters. Soon a man carrying a white flag walked alone toward the Alamo. He was admitted to see Colonel Travis.

The messenger brought a note from the Mexican commander. Though it was in the most courteous language, General Santa Anna demanded that the Alamo be surrendered at once. Otherwise, the fort would be blown to bits and its defenders "put to the sword." That was the way army commanders talked in those days. They meant it, too.

Colonel Travis was not nearly so polite as General Santa Anna. He sent the messenger back with a blunt reply in two words: "No surrender."

The messenger bowed and left the fort. He was given time to cross the quarter-mile of No Man's Land between fort and town. Then, an Alamo cannon boomed and sent a single shot into the enemy camp.

At the same instant, the Lone Star flag was

run quickly up a pole to flutter high above the Alamo's walls.

It was one of the great moments in American history.

Santa Anna's reply was prompt. A blood-red flag—meaning that no quarter would be given —raced up a pole at the Mexican army headquarters. A battery of artillery thundered into action. The Alamo shivered as big iron balls crashed against the walls, then bounced. A famous battle had begun.

It began badly so far as the Americans were concerned. Colonel Bowie, who had been ill for several days, was suddenly stricken. He could no longer walk. He was placed on a cot where he could watch the enemy.

The bombardment continued. Because the Americans were short of cannon balls, Colonel Travis told his men to use the artillery carefully, to fire only when a good target offered.

Colonel Crockett was all over the fort, watching every side. Now and then he helped the cannoneers to elevate a gun in order to reach supply trains bringing ammunition to the Mexicans. Again, he moved riflemen from one wall to another to pick off enemy artillerymen. Busy as he was, he had time to notice that his four strange companions were as brave as they were active.

With guns roaring and the Lone Star flag flying high, the Bee Hunter started singing, his clear voice cheering his comrades, his rifle firing at every opportunity. The old, old Indian, feeble as he was, took his turn shooting from the top of the walls. The Pirate, as it turned out, had had some experience with big guns in his day, and now he served with the Alamo artillery, his fierce black whiskers and red handkerchief adding a sort of Captain Kidd note to the defenders.

Thimblerig, of whom Crockett had had his doubts, proved to be recklessly brave. He spent most of his time exposed on the walls. During lulls in the shooting, he removed his tall white hat and played with the pea and thimbles. "Have to keep in practice," he said.

On the second day of the attack, Thimblerig came looking for Davy, his hands on his chest, blood oozing from between his fingers.

"Colonel," he complained, "those Mexicans don't like my hat. They missed it every time and got so mad they shot me."

Crockett examined the wound and, using his knife, extracted a three-ounce ball of lead from it. "You'll live, Thimblerig," he said, "but maybe you'd better leave your fine hat inside the fort." The lanky fellow returned to his place on the parapet.

Next day the Mexicans brought four more batteries into action, and after an hour's terrific bombardment, two regiments of infantry charged the fort. Crockett massed his best riflemen on that side and kept up such a hot fire that the Mexicans broke ranks and began fleeing. They were called back.

General Santa Anna saw that more preparation was needed before the little fort could be taken. During the night he had his artillery wheeled nearer. At dawn the guns opened fire at close range. The sides of the Alamo quickly showed the effects as bricks, hunks of mortar, and pieces of timber were blown into the air. The ground was soon covered with debris.

Again the defenders rallied on the parapet, picking off the mounted officers first, then directing their fire at the artillery. It was a terrible morning of noise and smoke and fire and death. A cannon ball sailed over and fell into the Alamo's parade ground. There it burst, killing two men and wounding two more.

For eleven days after the first shot, the Mexicans kept trying to capture the fort. Balls tore into the walls every hour, day and night. Again and again the brave Mexican troops attacked, only to be shot down with horrible losses.

Meanwhile, those within the fort were running out of ammunition.

Crockett went to Colonel Travis. He was cheerful, still joking in the Crockett manner. "Colonel," he said, "by tomorrow I'll be loading my rifle with nails. I've got two bullets left."

Travis was shocked. "Is it as bad as that?"

"It sure is. I'll be shooting nails tomorrow. The day after, I'll be shooting stones—if I can find any."

"Is everybody in the same fix?"

"I reckon the whole of us don't have more than two or three rounds a piece. That is, of lead. We've got plenty of powder but nothing to shoot with it."

Travis was ill, barely able to totter around with a rifle for a cane. But there was nothing the matter with his courage. He smiled. "Well," he said, "I'm glad the Mexicans don't know how bad off we are."

During the night the men in the fort heard increased activity among the enemy. Orders were being shouted. Troops could be heard moving about. Horses neighed. It sounded to Crockett, standing in the dark along the walls, as though more soldiers were being added to the enemy camp. "They'll try it again in the morning," he thought.

Crockett set men to searching the fort for pieces of metal that could be used for bullets. He cheered everybody, pausing once to tell a fantastic story about the time he "grinned" a laughing hyena in a circus until the animal wept. "Saddest sight I ever did see," he said.

The night wore on. There was little or no sleep within the fort. Like Bowie, Travis had now taken to a cot. Davy Crockett was asked to take command officially as colonel. He refused. "That's not necessary," he said. "All hands are doing as well as they can, and I'll just keep moving around."

The expected attack began with the first glimmer of light. A single bugle call set things going. Crockett took his place on the walls. Every rifleman was at his post. The fort's cannon were ready. Beside them were the gunners, the smoke from their slow-burning matches curling up.

The new attack started with a crashing volley of artillery fire, close enough to blast great holes in the walls. Between the volleys the defenders could hear a brass band playing. Somebody told Crockett the piece played was an old Spanish battle tune that meant "no mercy."

As the smoke billowed in clouds around the Mexicans, out of it came regiments of foot soldiers, all running double-quick toward the fort. On they came, rank after rank, each company carrying four long ladders.

Colonel Crockett passed an order down the line of his marksmen. "Get them fellers with the ladders." The Americans fired. A few laddermen fell. Other men took their places. On came the charge.

Just as the first wave of infantry reached the base of the wall, the enemy artillery opened up with a mighty barrage that dropped red hot balls into the fort. Smoke curled up where timbers started to burn.

Up went the ladders, and Mexican troops as brave as any soldiers that ever fought started upward into the very muzzles of the American rifles. A good half of them died before they were little more than off the ground, but their comrades gained the top of the wall.

At almost this same moment other Mexicans

Davy swung his rifle to topple the first Mexican he saw.

with a big battering ram went to work pounding the gates, smashing them in like so much cardboard. In another instant, more red hot balls dropped into the fort, fired by cannon that had been moved around to the northeast.

More ladders were leaned on the walls. Quick young Mexicans with swords or bayonetted carbines climbed them. Gunfire was of no use now. The Americans turned their rifles into clubs. Bowie knives came out of their belts, while James Bowie himself, half alive, watched from the last sick bed he would know.

Up onto the west parapet staggered Colonel Travis, weak from fever, his eyes set and staring, determined to strike one more blow. He helped to point a cannon, then called to Crockett. "Take the south wall. They're coming up there."

Davy turned. Just then Travis threw up his arms and fell dead on the parapet. Davy ran to the south wall. The Mexicans were coming, all right, coming up fast. He swung his rifle to topple the first Mexican he saw. Smoke was so thick he could see very little.

The enemy was now inside the fort below. They started up to take the Americans on the wall from behind. Probably they were shouting. No one could tell. There was too much other noise. The choking fumes of burning powder covered everything. Somewhere in the fury of smoke and noise Davy Crockett drew his knife and blindly lunged and slashed—and died. . . .

It was all over now. A strange hush fell upon the battered little fort that stood so lonely in the vast panorama that was Texas. A soft breeze slowly thinned the clouds of smoke, wafting them out over the miles of blue buffalo clover. The Alamo had fallen.

No American had tried to flee. No American survived. Just outside the fort, Mexican troops buried their own dead. Then they made a huge funeral pyre of wooden beams and planks. On top of this they laid the bodies of the American dead. They set it on fire. The flames leaped high, then fell, then rose again, burning throughout much of the night of March 6, 1836. By morning the pile of wood and bodies had been reduced to a blanket of gray ashes on the ground.

The Alamo had fallen, but taking it had delayed General Santa Anna a full twelve days.

That was enough to insure his eventual defeat. The Texas legislature meanwhile formally proclaimed Texas independence and also raised an army fit to take the field against the Mexicans.

Seven weeks later, under General Sam Houston, the Texans surprised Santa Anna's army at San Jacinto. They went into action shouting their incomparable battle cry—*Remember the Alamo!* They broke and scattered the Mexicans, and took their commander prisoner. The Texas Republic was assured. The fight at the Alamo had made it possible. Davy Crockett had died a hero among heroes as great as he.

MEMORIALS TO DAVY CROCKETT

CROCKETT IN TENNESSEE

The memory of no native son is more cherished in Tennessee than that of David Crockett. Should you plan a visit there, you might like to know there are two monuments to him in the state. One is a full-length statue in Lawrenceburg, the other a heroic-size bust in Trenton. There are also eight historical markers which call attention to people, places and scenes he knew well. Below is an official list, prepared by the State of Tennessee, of the Crockett markers and their locations.

DAVY CROCKETT'S BIRTHPLACE (US 11E), near underpass in the town of Limestone, Washington County. Where Limestone Creek joins the Nolichucky River is a slab of limestone marking the site of the cabin in which Crockett was born in 1786.

THE CROCKETT TAVERN (US 11E) in Morristown, Hamblen County. Here stood John Crockett's tavern where Davy spent a part of his boyhood.

DAVY CROCKETT'S HOMESTEAD (State 55) near bridge over Mulberry Creek, Moore County, three and a half miles northeast of Lynchburg. Site of log house he built and in which he lived from 1808 to 1812.

DAVY CROCKETT'S HOME (US 43 & 64) at 218 S. Military Street, Lawrenceburg, Lawrence County. Marker on site of home where he lived 1819-1822 when he became colonel of militia and member of the Tennessee legislature.

"KENTUCK" (US 64) two and three-tenths miles west of Belvidere, Franklin County, at road junction. Site of home Crockett occupied and named in 1812 is marked by a well in a field three and a half miles south and to the east of this road. From here Crockett went to the Creek War. His first wife died here.

POLLY FINLAY CROCKETT (US 64). At road junction in Maxwell, Franklin County, two and seven-tenths miles west of bridge in Belvidere. Crockett's first wife is buried in an old cemetery overlooking Bean's Creek, five miles to the southeast. She died in 1815 shortly after her husband returned from the Creek War.

CROCKETT's MILL (US 64) one hundred yards west of bridge over Shoal Creek, Lawrence County. Two miles north of here Crockett built a gristmill that was destroyed in 1821 by flood. He soon moved to West Tennessee.

REBECCA HAWKINS CROCKETT (US 45) in Rutherford, Gibson County. The mother of Davy Crockett is buried in a now unused cemetery in Tyson Store community, five and nine-tenths miles to the northwest. She came here with her son and died shortly after he left for Texas.

CROCKETT IN ALABAMA

On US 241 is the city of Talladega, site of the BATTLE OF FORT TALLADEGA, 1813, in which Crockett fought.

On US 43 in Franklin County is RUSSELL-VILLE, named for Major William Russell, the brave officer with whom Crockett served in the Creek War.

CROCKETT IN TEXAS

On US 287, in Houston County, is the town of CROCKETT, named for the Tennessean who camped here overnight on his way to The Alamo in 1836. His camp site is about 500 feet from Crockett Circle in the town. In Houston County and adjacent Trinity County is the CROCKETT NATIONAL FOREST, where Davy hunted game.

In west Texas, on US 290, is CROCKETT COUNTY, and a DAVID CROCKETT MONUMENT.

Not far from the center of San Antonio, on the east side of Alamo Plaza and shadowed by tall buildings, is perhaps the most celebrated battle site in all the Southwest. Here are the remains of the ALAMO fortress. A monument marks the center of the former fortress area. Davy Crockett is one of the central figures in the groups of soldiers on the sides of the monument. Near by is THE ALAMO MUSEUM.

Index

A

Alabama, 46, 49, 98, 124, 172
Alamo, 146, 153-68, 172-73
Alamo Museum, 173
Alamo Plaza, 172
Alligators, 44-45, 105-06
American settlements, 46
Arithmetic, 4
Arkansas River, 136
Arkansas Territory, 136-37
Austin, Moses, 134
Austin, Stephen, 134-35

B

Baltimore, Maryland, 20, 26
Barn raisings, 25
Barter system, 119
Bear episodes, 8-11, 43-44, 54-59, 107, 116-17
Bed, without supper, 4, 11-12
Bee Hunter, 140-42, 145, 147, 150, 160
Big Road, 18
Birds, 7-8
Blizzard, 18, 104-05

Blue Ridge Mountains, 19-21
Boston, Massachusetts, 129
Bowie, James, 145-46, 153-57,
    159, 163, 166
Bowie knife, 45, 166
British, 45-46
Buffalo, 148-50
Burleson, Edward, 146
Bushwhackers, 61

C

Cane brakes, 102-03
Cannon fire, 95
Carolina parakeets, 7-8
Carroll, William, 82, 86, 93-96
Casualties, 69
Cherokee Indians, 126, 133
Chickasaw Indians, 103
Choctaw Indians, 103
Ciphering, 4
Clark (woodsman), 28-29, 31
Coffee, John, 52-53, 55-56, 58,
    61-67, 69-71
Congress, 107, 116-17, 119-23,
    127, 130-31, 133
Coonskin caps, 119
Coosa River, 61-62, 69
Creek Indians, 46, 49-52, 61-79,
    81, 84-86, 88-91, 93-98,
    126, 134, 171
Crockett, David:
  ancestry, 13
  appearance, 26, 30
  at 8, 3, 12, 27, 58
  at 10, 58
  at 12, 14-15
  at 50, 14
  bad habits, 25
  birth, 13, 170
  birthplace, 170
  "bound out", 14-15
  boyhood, 14-23
  bragging, 31
  business, 101

children, 37, 39, 41, 46-47,
    99, 103-04
colonelcy, 100, 170
Congress, election to, 122-23,
    127, 133
death, 167-68
education, 19, 23-25
feinting, 50
grin, 44-45, 163
height, 6, 26
Indians, attitude toward, 99,
    103, 119-31, 134
judgeship, 100
legend, 130
"life", 17
marriage, 36-37
marriage (2nd), 99-100
marriage plans, 26-27, 32-34
memorials, 169-73
memory, 25
motto, 100, 126
reading, 100
representative, 101, 106, 170
rule for himself, 64
shooting matches, 27-32
sibling sequence, 13
stories, 101, 104-06
ventriloquism, 121
wife's death, 99
writing, 25, 100
Crockett, David (grandfather),
    13, 47
Crockett, John (father), 4, 13-
    14, 16, 19, 22, 24, 47
Crockett, John (son), 99
Crockett, Mrs. David (1st wife),
    36-43, 46-47, 81, 99, 171
Crockett, Mrs. David (2nd
    wife), 99-101
Crockett, Polly (daughter), 99
Crockett, Rebecca Hawkins
    (mother), 13, 171
Crockett, Robbie (son), 104-05
Crockett, William (son), 99,
    104, 130, 133
Crockett, Texas, 172

Crockett, cabin, 6
Crockett County, Texas, 172
Crockett National Forest, 172
Crockett tavern, 14-16, 19, 22,
    27, 37, 170
Crockett's mill, 171

D

Dances, 25-26
Devil's Elbow, 114
Dogs, 47, 103, 116
Drover, 15, 19
Duels, 129-30

E

Earthquakes, 102
Education, 4
Elk River, 42
Enlistment period, 79
Evans, Captain, 74-76, 78

F

Farming, 15, 20, 22
Field music, 57
Finlay, Polly, 26, 32-34, 35-37
Flintlock (rifle), 4-6
Florida, 98, 124
Food, 53, 56, 65
Fort Mims, 46-47, 49, 55
Franklin (State of), 13
Front Royal, 20
Fulton, 137
Furloughs, 79-81

G

Gamblers, 136
Georgia, 98, 124
Gibson County, 103
Gold, 124
Goliad, 156-57
Grist mill, 101

H

Hamblen County, 170
Hammond, Captain, 74-77
Holston River, 14, 16-17, 21,
    32, 39, 41
Honey, 43
Horseshoe Bend (battle), 97
Hounds, 47, 103, 116
Houston, Sam, 135, 146, 148
Houston County, Texas, 172
Hunter (steamer), 132
Hunting grounds, 98, 125, 134
Huntsman, Adam, 133

I

Indian(s), 13, 46, 98-99, 103,
    119-31, 146, 148, 160
Indian lands, 124-27, 129
Ireland, 13
Iron, use of, 108

J

Jackson, Andrew, 49-56, 58-62,
    69-70, 72-74, 78-82, 84-88,
    90-91, 94, 98, 122, 124-27,
    129
Johnson, Milo, 28-31

K

Kennedy, John, 22-26, 34, 37
King's Mountain (battle), 47

L

Lafitte, Jean, 148
Lawrenceburg, Tennessee, 169-
70
Limestone, Tennessee, 170
Limestone Creek, 170
Limestone River, 8
Lincoln County, 42, 44
Lion of the West (play), 130

Little Rock, Arkansas, 136-37
Lone Star flag, 158-60
Lone Star Republic. *See* Texas
Louisville, Kentucky, 132

M

Manhood, 8
Marksmanship, 4
Mayfield, George, 97
Memorials, 169-73
Memphis, 116
Mexican(s), 146-47, 151-52, 159-62, 164, 166-68
Mexican Army, 155-64
Mexico, 134-35
Military law, 80
Mills Point, 133, 135
Mississippi (State), 124
Mississippi River, 102, 109-17, 125, 136
Mississippi Territory, 46, 49, 88
Moore County, 170
Morristown, Tennessee, 170
Mulberry Creek, 170
Mulberry Fork, 42, 44
Muscle Shoals, 82

N

Nacogdoches, 143, 145, 147
Natchitoches, 137, 140
New England, 133
New Orleans, 109, 114
New York City, 129
Nolichucky Valley, 13, 170

O

Obion River, 102-03, 109, 116, 133, 135
Old Betsy (rifle), 27, 30-31, 37, 50, 116
"Old Hickory." *See* Jackson, Andrew
Opposum, 43-44

P

Parakeets, 7-8
Parrot family, 7
Patton, Mrs. Elizabeth, 99-100
Pea trick, 138-39
Philadelphia, 129, 136
Pirate, 148, 151-52, 160
Pittsburgh, 132
Possums, 104
Powder horn, 5
Provisions, 53, 56, 104, 157
Public lands, 123, 129

R

Rabbit snaring, 21-22
Raccoons, 104, 119
Red River, 137, 139
Redsticks. *See* Creek Indians
Revolutionary War, 13
Rifles, 4-6, 129, 135
Russell, William, 48, 51-54, 58, 61-63, 65-66, 70-72, 75-79, 82-88, 90-91, 93-95, 98-99, 172
Russellville, Alabama, 172

S

Sabine River, 143
San Antonio de Bexar, 145-47, 150-51, 153, 157, 172
San Jacinto (battle), 168
Santa Anna, General, 155-59, 161, 167
Sawyers, 110-11
Scouting period, 48-59
Shakes (The), 103, 105-06, 117, 120-21, 127
Shawnee Indians, 46
Shenandoah Valley, 15
Shooting matches, 27-32
Siler, Jacob, 15-18
Slave business, 107-09, 115-16
Snapping turtles, 102

Snow, 18-19
Spanish Trail (Old), 143
Speculators, 123, 133
Stevens, Lieutenant, 56

T

Talladega (fort), 70-71, 73-83, 172
Tallapoosa River, 62, 82-96
Tallushatches (camp), 63
Tecumseh (leader), 46
Tennessee, 13, 15-16, 30, 32, 37-38, 42, 44, 46, 54, 82, 102, 121, 127, 133-35, 145
Tennessee legislature, 101, 106
Tennessee River, 41, 52, 82
Texas, 134-35, 137, 140-42, 144-53, 156-57, 167-68, 172
Thimbling, 138-41, 145, 147, 160-61
Travis, William, 146, 153, 155-59, 162-63, 166
Trenton, Tennessee, 170
Trinity County, Texas, 172

Trinity River, 147
Turtles, 102

V

Virginia, 15, 19-20

W

Wagoners, 15-19, 21
War of 1812, 45
Washington, D. C., 119, 122, 127, 130
Water, transportation of, 108
"We're on our way to Baltimore", 89
Whale, Captain, 109, 111-13, 115
Whig Party, 127, 129
White River, 136
Wilson, Abraham, 22
Winchester, Major, 116
Winchester (trading center), 46-47, 81
Working bees, 25